cook's library
Chocolate

cook's library
Chocolate

p

This is a Parragon Book
First published in 2003

Parragon
Queen Street House
4 Queen Street
Bath BA1 1HE, UK

ISBN: 0-75258-755-2

Printed in China

NOTE

This book uses metric and imperial measurements. Follow the same
units of measurement throughout; do not mix metric and imperial.
All spoon measurements are level: teaspoons are assumed to be 5 ml,
and tablespoons are assumed to be 15 ml. Unless otherwise stated,
milk is assumed to be full fat, eggs and individual vegetables such as
potatoes are medium, and pepper is freshly ground black pepper.

The times given for each recipe are an approximate guide only because the
preparation times may differ according to the techniques used by different
people and the cooking times may vary as a result of the type of oven used.
The preparation times include chilling and marinating times, where appropriate.

Recipes using raw or very lightly cooked eggs should be
avoided by infants, the elderly, pregnant women, convalescents,
and anyone suffering from an illness.

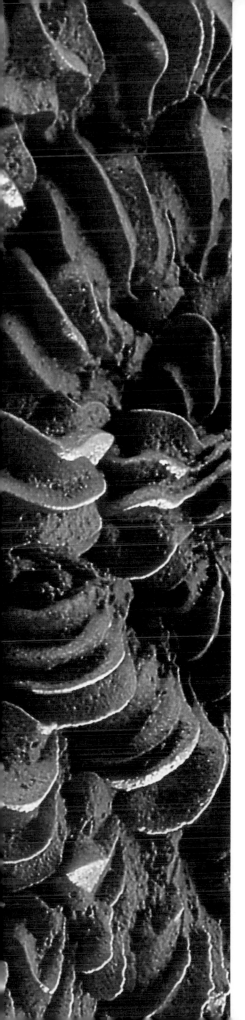

Contents

Introduction

Chocolate! – even the word is an enticing mixture of indulgence tinged with a touch of sinfulness, and the product itself more than lives up to its promise. The mere mention of anything associated with this mouthwatering confection can cause a dreamy look to come into the eyes of the chocoholic.

The cocoa tree, *Theobroma cacao*, originated in South America, and from the early 7th century it was cultivated by the Maya, who established a flourishing trade and even used the cocoa bean as currency. In 1502, Christopher Columbus took the cocoa bean to Spain, but it wasn't until later that Cortés introduced xocotlatl, a recipe brought from the Mexican court of Montezuma for a drink made of crushed roasted cocoa beans and cold water, thickened with cornflour and frothed with a swizzle stick. Vanilla, spices, honey and sugar were added to improve the flavour of this thick and bitter brew, and over time it came to be served hot. Cocoa was believed to cure a variety of physical illnesses and to promote stamina.

In the 17th century, the popularity of cocoa spread to the rest of Europe. France was the first country to fall to its charms, then Holland, where Amsterdam became the most important cocoa port beyond Spain. From there cocoa went to Germany, then north to Scandinavia, and also south to Italy – by which time it had become a major source of revenue.

Cocoa arrived in England in the mid-17th century, and chocolate houses quickly began to rival the newly established coffee houses.

In the early 19th century, Dutch chemist Coenraad Van Houten invented a press to extract the fat from the beans, and developed a method of neutralizing the acids. In this way, he was able to produce almost pure cocoa butter, and a hard 'cake', which could be milled to a powder for use as a flavouring. As a result, it became possible to eat chocolate as well as to drink it.

It was soon discovered that the rich cocoa butter made a delicious confection, and chocolate production began in earnest. In Britain, Fry's chocolate appeared in 1847, and in Switzerland the famous chocolate companies were established. In 1875 chocolate was combined with condensed milk to produce the first milk chocolate. At around this time, Lindt found a way of making the smooth, melting chocolate still associated with his company today. About 20 years later, Hershey introduced his famous chocolate bar in the United States, where chocolate is perhaps better loved than anywhere else.

Today, cocoa trees are grown in Africa, the West Indies, the tropical areas of America, and the Far East. Harvested cocoa beans are left in the heat of the sun to develop their chocolate flavour, then afterwards the beans are shelled, and the kernels are processed to produce cocoa solids. Finally, the cocoa butter is extracted and further processed to become chocolate, in all its many guises.

Regional Cooking

The Europeans, following their long association with cocoa as a drink, soon discovered the delights of chocolate, and set about using it to create some of the most delicious classic dessert recipes – rich, creamy, and incredibly good to eat.

In Austria, tortes are very popular, particularly Anna Sacher's delectable Sachertorte, which dates from 1883. The French offer a melting Chocolate Roulade, a light-as-air mixture that is cooked in a long rectangle, then rolled around a filling – there is plenty of scope for variations on this basic recipe. Also from France comes Chocolate Mousse, a melt-in-the-mouth dessert based on chocolate and eggs, to which can be added double cream, brandy, rum – or even Champagne.

The Italians really know how to impress with their chocolate desserts. Chocolate Zabaglione, laced with Marsala, is whisked over hot water until thick, and served immediately – so it needs patient guests and a confident cook! Tiramisu is based on a smooth and versatile cream cheese, mascarpone, which is layered with coffee-drenched sponge and chunks of chocolate. And the Italians are, of course, wonderful at making ice cream – the combination of chocolate and mint is a classic favourite. For special occasions, two Tuscan specialities are Panforte di Siena – a rich, cocoa-flavoured mixture of dried fruit, nuts, spices and honey – and Florentines – thin, crispy biscuits topped with chocolate.

From Germany comes the Black Forest Gâteau, a chocolate cake soaked in liqueur and filled with whipped cream and cherries. Adapted into a trifle, this makes a very special dessert.

It may seem a strange and newly fashionable idea to combine the creamy sweetness of chocolate with the hot and fiery chilli, but in fact chilli was one of the flavourings used in the original cocoa drink, Xocotlatl, and the combination is still used in Mexican cooking today. That chocolate and chilli have an affinity is evident in one of the most popular Mexican dishes, Mole Poblano, a blend of toasted fresh chillies, onions, garlic, tomatoes, spices, nuts, raisins – and chocolate, which is even used to garnish the dish. Chocolate also adds flavour and richness to Mexican Beef Stew.

More conventionally, chocolate is used in desserts such as Empanadas, little parcels of banana and chocolate in filo pastry, and Chocolate Meringues, served with strawberries and chocolate-flavoured cream. The Mexicans also make a modern version of the original cocoa drink, which is spiced with cinnamon and thickened with tortilla flour.

In North America, where home-baked cookies and traybakes are such a feature of everyday life and social occasions, chocolate is a very popular ingredient. From here come such tempting treats as the moist, chewy Chocolate Brownie, Chocolate Crispy Bites, and Rocky Road Bites, which often find their way into ice cream. Some recipes reflect the area in which a recipe originated – one that particularly catches the attention is Mississippi Mud Pie, definitely not a dish for the faint-hearted! And Devil's Food Cake, with its sumptuous chocolate frosting, is just as the name suggests – positively wicked!

How to Use Chocolate

Chocolate is delicious whether cooked or uncooked. It comes in many forms and here is a selection of some of the most popular types, which can all be used in a wide variety of mouthwatering recipes.

Dark Chocolate

Dark chocolate that contains around 50% cocoa solids is ideal for most everyday cooking purposes. For special recipes, choose a luxury or continental chocolate with a cocoa solid content of 70–75% for a richer, more intense flavour.

White Chocolate

For colour contrast, especially for cake decoration, white chocolate is unbeatable. However, white chocolate has a lower content of cocoa butter and cocoa solids, so choose a luxury cooking variety and take care not to overheat it when melting it.

Chocolate Chips

Available in dark, milk or white varieties, these small pieces of chocolate are immensely useful for baking and decoration. They are especially good in biscuits and cookies, as well as sweets, breads, rolls and a whole range of delicious confections.

Milk Chocolate

This variety has a milder, creamier flavour. It is also useful for decorations. Care must be taken when melting it, however, because milk chocolate is more sensitive to heat than dark chocolate is.

Cocoa Powder

Cocoa powder should be bought unsweetened. It tastes bitter, and gives a good, strong chocolate flavour in cooking. It is mostly used in cakes.

Chocolate-flavoured Cake Covering

This product has an inferior flavour, but it is extremely useful for making decorations because of its high fat content. As a compromise, add a few squares to a good-quality chocolate.

🍳 COOK'S TIP

Most chocolate, including cocoa powder, can be stored for up to a year if it is kept in a cool, dry place away from direct heat or sunlight.

Preparing Chocolate

To melt chocolate on a stove:

1 Break the chocolate into small, equal-sized pieces and put it into a heatproof bowl.

2 Place the bowl over a pan of hot but not boiling water, making sure the base of the bowl does not come into contact with the water.

3 Once the chocolate starts to melt, stir gently until smooth, then remove from the heat.

Note: Do not melt chocolate over direct heat (unless melting with other ingredients – in this case, keep the heat very low).

To melt chocolate in a microwave oven:

1 Break chocolate into small pieces and place them in a microwave-proof bowl.

2 Put the bowl in the microwave oven and melt. As a guide, melt 125g/4½ oz dark chocolate on High for 2 minutes, and white or milk chocolate on Medium for 2–3 minutes.

Note: As microwave oven temperatures and settings vary, you should consult the manufacturer's instructions first.

3 Stir the chocolate, leave to stand for a few minutes, then stir again. If necessary, return it to the microwave for a further 30 seconds.

Chocolate Decorations

Decorations add a special touch to a cake or dessert. They can be interleaved with non-stick baking paper and stored in airtight containers. Dark chocolate will keep for 4 weeks, and milk or white chocolate for 2 weeks.

Caraque

1 Spread the melted chocolate over a clean acrylic chopping board and leave it to set.

2 When the chocolate has set, hold the board firmly, position a large, smooth-bladed knife on the chocolate and pull the blade towards you at an angle of 45°, scraping along the chocolate to form the caraque. You should end up with irregularly shaped long curls (see below).

3 Using the knife blade, lift the caraque off the board.

Quick Curls

1 For quick curls, choose a thick bar of chocolate, and keep it at room temperature.

2 Using a sharp, swivel-bladed vegetable peeler, scrape lightly along the chocolate to form fine curls, or more firmly to form thicker curls.

Leaves

1 Use freshly picked leaves with well-defined veins that are clean, dry and pliable. Holding a leaf by its stem, paint a smooth layer of melted chocolate on to the underside with a small paint brush or pastry brush.

2 Repeat with the remaining leaves, then place them, chocolate side up, on a baking sheet lined with silicone paper.

3 Chill in the refrigerator for at least an hour until set. When set, peel each leaf away from its chocolate coating.

How to Use This Book

Each recipe contains a wealth of useful information, including preparation and cooking times, and level of difficulty. All of this information is explained in detail below.

A full-colour photograph of the finished dish.

The ingredients for each recipe are listed in the order that they are used.

The method is clearly explained with step-by-step instructions that are easy to follow.

Cook's tips provide useful information regarding ingredients or hints on cooking techniques.

⭐ The number of stars represents the difficulty of each recipe, ranging from very easy (1 star) to challenging (4 stars).

🕐 This amount of time represents the preparation of ingredients, including cooling, chilling and soaking times.

🕐 This represents the cooking time.

Cakes, Gâteaux *and* Loaves

It is hard to resist the pleasure of a sumptuous piece of chocolate cake and no chocolate book would be complete without a selection of cakes, gâteaux and loaves – there are plenty to choose from in this chapter. The more experimental among you can vary the fillings or decorations according to what takes your fancy. Alternatively, follow our easy step-by-step instructions and look at our glossy pictures to guide you to perfect results.

The gâteaux in this book are a feast for the eyes; and so are the delicious cakes, many of which can be made with surprising ease. The loaves are the perfect indulgence for teatime and can be made with very little effort. So next time you feel like a mouthwatering slice of something, these recipes are sure to be a success.

This is a good family cake that keeps well. Baked in a shallow rectangular cake tin, it is ideal for selling at a cake stall or charity coffee morning.

Chocolate Tray Bake

SERVES 15

350 g/12 oz self-raising flour, sifted
3 tbsp cocoa powder, sifted
225 g/8 oz caster sugar
225 g/8 oz soft margarine
4 eggs, beaten
4 tbsp milk
50 g/1¾ oz milk chocolate chips
50 g/1¾ oz dark chocolate chips
50 g/1¾ oz white chocolate chips
icing sugar, to dust

1 Grease a 33 x 23 x 5-cm/13 x 9 x 2-inch cake tin.

2 Place all of the ingredients except for the chocolate chips and icing sugar in a large mixing bowl and beat together until smooth.

3 Beat in the milk, dark and white chocolate chips.

4 Spoon the mixture into the prepared cake tin and level the top. Bake in a preheated oven, 180°C/350°F/Gas Mark 4, for 30–40 minutes, until risen and springy to the touch. Leave to cool in the tin.

5 Once cool, dust with icing sugar. Cut into squares to serve.

very easy

10 mins

30–40 mins

ⓦ COOK'S TIP

For an attractive finish, cut thin strips of paper and lay them in a criss-cross pattern across the top of the cake. Dust lightly with icing sugar, then gently remove the paper strips.

Decorated with thick yogurt and canned pineapple, this is a low-fat cake, but it is by no means lacking in flavour.

Chocolate *and* Pineapple Cake

1 Lightly grease a 20-cm/8-inch square cake tin.

2 Place the low-fat spread, caster sugar, flour, cocoa powder, baking powder and eggs in a large mixing bowl. Beat with a wooden spoon or electric hand whisk until smooth.

3 Pour the cake mixture into the prepared tin and level the surface. Bake in a preheated oven, 190°C/375°F/Gas Mark 5, for 20–25 minutes or until springy to the touch. Leave the cake to cool slightly in the tin before transferring to a wire rack to cool completely.

4 Drain the pineapple, chop the pineapple pieces and drain again. Reserve a little pineapple for decoration, then stir the rest into the yogurt and sweeten to taste with icing sugar.

5 Spread the pineapple and yogurt mixture over the cake and decorate with the reserved pineapple pieces. Sprinkle with the grated chocolate.

SERVES 9

150 g/5½ oz low-fat spread
125 g/4½ oz caster sugar
100 g/3½ oz self-raising flour, sifted
3 tbsp cocoa powder, sifted
1½ tsp baking powder
2 eggs
225 g/8 oz canned pineapple pieces in natural juice
125 ml/4 fl oz low-fat thick natural yogurt
about 1 tbsp icing sugar
grated chocolate, to decorate

 COOK'S TIP

Store the cake, undecorated, in an airtight container for up to 3 days. Once decorated, refrigerate and use within 2 days.

★★   easy
🕐   40 mins
🕐   20–25 mins

An all-time favourite combination of flavours makes this cake ideal for a teatime treat. Omit the icing, if preferred, and sprinkle with icing sugar.

Chocolate *and* Orange Cake

SERVES 8

175 g/6 oz caster sugar
175 g/6 oz butter or block margarine
3 eggs, beaten
175 g/6 oz self-raising flour, sifted
2 tbsp cocoa powder, sifted
2 tbsp milk
3 tbsp orange juice
grated rind of ½ orange

icing
175 g/6 oz icing sugar
2 tbsp orange juice

1 Lightly grease a 20-cm/8-inch deep round cake tin.

2 Beat together the sugar and butter in a bowl until light and fluffy. Gradually add the eggs, beating well after each addition. Carefully fold in the flour.

3 Divide the cake mixture in half. Add the cocoa powder and milk to one half, stirring until well combined. Flavour the other half of the mixture with the orange juice and rind.

4 Place spoonfuls of each mixture into the prepared tin and swirl together with a skewer to create a marbled effect. Bake in a preheated oven, 190°C/375°F/Gas Mark 5, for 25 minutes or until springy to the touch.

5 Leave the cake to cool in the tin for a few minutes before transferring to a wire rack to cool completely.

6 To make the icing, sift the icing sugar into a mixing bowl and mix in enough of the orange juice to form a smooth icing. Spread the icing over the top of the cake, decorate with feather icing (see Cook's Tip) and leave to set.

⭐⭐   easy

1 hr

25 mins

🍳 COOK'S TIP

For feather icing, pipe parallel lines of chocolate icing or melted chocolate across the cake. Draw a cocktail stick across the lines at right angles, alternating the direction of your pull.

An easy-to-make family cake ideal for a treat. Keep the decoration as simple as you like – you could use a shop-bought icing or filling, if preferred.

Family Chocolate Cake

1 Lightly grease two 18-cm/7-inch shallow cake tins.

2 Place all of the ingredients for the cake in a large mixing bowl and beat with a wooden spoon or electric hand whisk to form a smooth mixture.

3 Divide the mixture between the prepared tins and level the tops. Bake in a preheated oven, 190°C/375°F/Gas Mark 5, for 20 minutes or until springy to the touch. Cool for a few minutes in the tins before transferring to a wire rack to cool completely.

4 To make the filling, beat the icing sugar and butter together in a bowl until light and fluffy. Melt the cooking chocolate and beat half into the mixture. Use the filling to sandwich the 2 cakes together.

5 Spread the remaining melted cooking chocolate over the top of the cake. Pipe circles of contrasting melted milk or white chocolate and feather into the cooking chocolate with a cocktail stick, if liked (see Cook's Tip on page 22). Leave to set before serving.

SERVES **8**

125 g/4½ oz soft margarine
125 g/4½ oz caster sugar
2 eggs
1 tbsp golden syrup
125 g/4½ oz self-raising flour, sifted
2 tbsp cocoa powder, sifted

filling and topping
50 g/1¾ oz icing sugar, sifted
2 tbsp butter
100 g/3½ oz white or milk cooking chocolate
a little milk or white chocolate, melted (optional)

COOK'S TIP

This cake is at its best when freshly made.

easy

1 hr

20 mins

An old-fashioned favourite, this cake will keep well if stored in an airtight container or wrapped in foil in a cool place.

Chocolate *and* Vanilla Loaf

SERVES 10

175 g/6 oz caster sugar
175 g/6 oz soft margarine
½ tsp vanilla essence
3 eggs
225 g/8 oz self-raising flour, sifted
50 g/1¾ oz dark chocolate, melted
icing sugar, to dust

1 Lightly grease a 450-g/1-lb loaf tin.

2 Beat together the sugar and soft margarine in a bowl until light and fluffy.

3 Beat in the vanilla essence, then gradually add the eggs, beating well after each addition. Carefully fold in the self-raising flour.

4 Divide the mixture in half. Stir the dark chocolate into one half of the mixture until well combined.

5 Place the vanilla mixture in the tin and level the top. Spread the chocolate layer over the vanilla layer.

6 Bake in a preheated oven, 190°C/ 375°F/Gas Mark 5, for 30 minutes or until springy to the touch.

7 Leave to cool in the tin for a few minutes before transferring to a wire rack to cool completely.

8 Serve the loaf dusted with icing sugar.

⊛ **COOK'S TIP**

Freeze the cake undecorated for up to 2 months. Defrost at room temperature.

very easy

50 mins

30 mins

What can be better in the afternoon than sitting down with a cup of tea and a slice of tea bread made with chocolate?

Chocolate Tea Bread

1 Lightly grease a 900-g/2-lb loaf tin and line the base with baking paper.

2 Cream together the butter and sugar in a bowl until light and fluffy.

3 Gradually add the eggs, beating well after each addition. If the mixture begins to curdle, beat in 1–2 tablespoons of the flour.

4 Stir in the chocolate chips, raisins, walnuts and orange rind. Fold in the flour. Spoon the mixture into the prepared loaf tin and make a slight dip in the centre of the top with the back of a spoon.

5 Bake in a preheated oven, 170°C / 325°F/Gas Mark 3, for 1 hour or until a fine skewer inserted into the centre of the loaf comes out clean.

6 Leave to cool in the tin for 5 minutes before carefully turning out and leaving on a wire rack to cool completely.

SERVES 4

175 g/6 oz butter, softened
100 g/3½ oz light muscovado sugar
4 eggs, beaten lightly
225 g/8 oz self-raising flour, sifted
225 g/8 oz dark chocolate chips
100 g/3½ oz raisins
50 g/1¾ oz chopped walnuts
finely grated rind of 1 orange

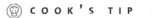 **COOK'S TIP**

Use white or milk chocolate chips instead of dark chocolate chips, or a mixture of all three, if desired. Dried cranberries instead of the raisins also work well in this recipe.

 ★★★   moderate

🕐   45 mins

🕐   1 hr

Chocolate cake and a creamy coffee-flavoured filling are combined in this delicious mocha cake.

Mocha Layer Cake

SERVES 8

200 g/7 oz self-raising flour
¼ tsp baking powder
4 tbsp cocoa powder
100 g/3½ oz caster sugar
2 eggs
2 tbsp golden syrup
150 ml/5 fl oz sunflower oil
150 ml/5 fl oz milk

filling

1 tsp instant coffee
1 tbsp boiling water
300 ml/10 fl oz double cream
2 tbsp icing sugar

to decorate

50 g/1¾ oz Quick Curls (see page 15)
  or grated chocolate
Caraque (see page 15)
icing sugar, to dust

1 Lightly grease three 18-cm/7-inch cake tins.

2 Sift the flour, baking powder and cocoa powder into a large mixing bowl. Stir in the sugar. Make a well in the centre and put in the eggs, syrup, oil and milk. Beat the liquids with a wooden spoon, gradually mixing in the dry ingredients to make a smooth mixture. Divide the mixture between the prepared tins.

3 Bake in a preheated oven, 180°C/ 350°F/Gas Mark 4, for 35–45 minutes or until springy to the touch. Leave in the tins for 5 minutes, then turn out on to wire racks to cool completely.

4 Dissolve the instant coffee in the boiling water and place in a bowl with the cream and icing sugar. Whip until the cream is just holding its shape. Use half of the cream to sandwich the 3 cakes together.

5 Transfer to a serving plate. Spread the remaining cream over the top and sides of the cake. Lightly press the chocolate curls or grated chocolate into the cream around the edge of the cake. Lay the caraque over the top. Cut a few thin strips of baking paper and place on top of the caraque. Dust lightly with icing sugar, then carefully remove the paper. Chill until ready to serve.

moderate

50 mins

35–45 mins

Thin layers of delicious light chocolate cake are sandwiched together with a rich chocolate icing.

Rich Chocolate Layer Cake

1 Grease a deep 23 cm/9-inch square cake tin and then line the base with baking paper.

2 Whisk the eggs and caster sugar together in a mixing bowl with an electric whisk for about 10 minutes or until the mixture is very thick. Lift the whisk up and let the mixture drizzle back – it will leave a trail for a few seconds when thick enough.

3 Sift the flour and cocoa together and fold half into the mixture. Drizzle over the melted butter and fold in with the rest of the flour and cocoa. Pour into the prepared tin and bake in a preheated oven, 180°C/350°F/Gas Mark 4, for 30–35 minutes or until springy to the touch. Leave to cool slightly, then remove from the tin and cool completely on a wire rack.

4 Melt the chocolate and butter together, then remove from the heat. Stir in the icing sugar, leave to cool, then beat until thick enough to spread.

5 Halve the cooled cake lengthways and cut each half into 3 layers. Sandwich the layers together with three-quarters of the chocolate filling. Spread the remainder over the cake and mark a wavy pattern on the top. Press the almonds on to the sides. Decorate with chocolate curls or grated chocolate.

SERVES 10

7 eggs
200 g/7 oz caster sugar
150 g/5½ oz plain flour
50 g/1¾ oz cocoa powder
4 tbsp butter, melted

filling

200 g/7 oz dark chocolate
125 g/4½ oz butter
4 tbsp icing sugar

to decorate

75 g/2¾ oz toasted flaked almonds, crushed lightly
chocolate Quick Curls (see page 15) or grated chocolate

 COOK'S TIP

When folding in dry ingredients, use a metal spoon and turn it in a gentle figure-of-eight movement until they are incorporated.

★★★   moderate

1 hr 5 mins

30–35 mins

This is an American classic, consisting of a rich, melt-in-the-mouth chocolate cake and a tangy citrus-flavoured frosting.

Devil's Food Cake

SERVES 6

250 g/9 oz self-raising flour
1 tsp bicarbonate of soda
225 g/8 oz butter
400 g/14 oz dark muscovado sugar
1 tsp vanilla essence
3 eggs
100 g/3½ oz dark chocolate, melted
125 ml/4 fl oz buttermilk
225 ml/8 fl oz boiling water
candied orange peel, to decorate

frosting
300 g/10½ oz caster sugar
2 egg whites
1 tbsp lemon juice
3 tbsp orange juice

1 Lightly grease two 20-cm/8-inch shallow round cake tins and line the bases with baking paper. Sift the flour and bicarbonate of soda together.

2 Beat the butter and sugar together in a bowl until pale and fluffy. Beat in the vanilla essence and the eggs, one at a time and beating well after each addition. Add a little flour to the mixture if it begins to curdle.

3 Fold the melted chocolate into the mixture until well blended. Gradually fold in the flour, then stir in the buttermilk and boiling water.

4 Divide the mixture between the tins and level the tops. Bake in a preheated oven, 190°C/375°F/Gas Mark 5, for 30 minutes, until springy to the touch. Leave to cool in the tin for 5 minutes, then transfer to a wire rack and leave to cool completely.

5 Place the frosting ingredients in a large bowl set over a pan of gently simmering water. Whisk, preferably with an electric beater, until thickened and forming soft peaks. Remove from the heat and whisk until the mixture is cool.

6 Sandwich the 2 cakes together with a little of the frosting, then spread the remainder over the top and sides of the cake, swirling it as you do so. Decorate with the candied orange peel.

moderate

1 hr

30 mins

What could be nicer than passion cake with added chocolate? Rich and moist, this cake is fabulous with afternoon tea.

Chocolate Passion Cake

1 Lightly grease the base of a deep 20-cm/ 8-inch round cake tin and line it with baking paper.

2 Place the eggs and caster sugar in a large bowl set over a pan of gently simmering water and whisk until very thick. Lift the whisk up and let the mixture drizzle – it will leave a trail for a few seconds when thick enough.

3 Remove the bowl from the heat. Sift the flour and cocoa powder into the bowl and carefully fold in. Fold in the carrots, walnuts and sunflower oil until just combined.

4 Pour into the prepared tin and bake in a preheated oven, 190°C/375°F/Gas Mark 5, for 45 minutes. Leave to cool slightly, then turn out on to a wire rack to cool completely.

5 Beat together the soft cheese and icing sugar until combined. Beat in the melted chocolate. Split the cake in half and sandwich together again with half of the chocolate mixture. Cover the top of the cake with the remainder of the chocolate mixture, swirling it with a knife. Chill or serve at once.

SERVES 6

5 eggs
150 g/5½ oz caster sugar
150 g/5½ oz plain flour
40 g/1½ oz cocoa powder
175 g/6 oz carrots, peeled, grated finely and squeezed until dry
50 g/1¾ oz chopped walnuts
2 tbsp sunflower oil

filling and topping
350 g/12 oz medium fat soft cheese
175 g/6 oz icing sugar
175 g/6 oz milk or dark chocolate, melted

🍳 COOK'S TIP

The undecorated cake can be frozen for up to 2 months. Defrost at room temperature for 3 hours or overnight in the refrigerator.

 moderate

45 mins

45 mins

CHOCOLATE

Adding yogurt to the cake mixture gives this baked chocolate cake a deliciously moist texture.

Chocolate Yogurt Cake

SERVES 8

150 ml/5 fl oz vegetable oil
150 ml/5 fl oz whole milk natural yogurt
175 g/6 oz light muscovado sugar
3 eggs, beaten
100 g/3½ oz wholemeal self-raising flour
125 g/4½ oz self-raising flour
2 tbsp cocoa powder
1 tsp bicarbonate of soda
50 g/1¾ oz dark chocolate, melted

filling and topping
150 ml/5 fl oz whole milk natural yogurt
150 ml/5 fl oz double cream
225 g/8 oz fresh soft fruit, such as strawberries or raspberries

1 Grease a deep 23-cm/9-inch round cake tin and line the base with baking paper.

2 Place the oil, yogurt, sugar and beaten eggs in a large mixing bowl and beat together until well combined. Sift the flours, cocoa powder and bicarbonate of soda together and beat into the yogurt mixture until well combined. Beat in the melted chocolate.

3 Pour into the prepared tin and bake in a preheated oven, 180°C/350°F/Gas Mark 4, for 45–50 minutes or until a fine skewer inserted into the centre comes out clean. Leave to cool in the tin for 5 minutes, then turn out on to a wire rack to cool completely. When cold, split the cake into 3 layers.

4 To make the filling, place the yogurt and cream in a large mixing bowl and whisk well until the mixture stands in soft peaks.

5 Place one layer of cake on a serving plate and spread with some of the cream. Top with a little of the fruit (slicing larger fruit such as strawberries). Repeat with the next layer. Top with the final layer of cake and spread with the rest of the cream. Top with more fruit and chill until ready to serve.

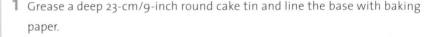

COOK'S TIP

When slicing a cake into layers, use a serrated knife in a gentle, sawing motion to avoid breaking up the crumb.

easy

55 mins

45–50 mins

This unusual cake is very popular with children, who love the appearance of the layers when it is sliced.

Chocolate Layer Log

1 Grease and line the sides of two 400-g/14-oz food cans.

2 Beat together the margarine and sugar in a bowl until light and fluffy. Gradually add the eggs, beating well after each addition. Sift together the flour and cocoa powder and fold into the cake mixture. Fold in the milk.

3 Divide the mixture between the two prepared cans. Stand the cans on a baking tray and bake in a preheated oven, 180°C/350°F/Gas Mark 4, for 40 minutes or until springy to the touch. Leave to cool for about 5 minutes in the cans, then turn out and leave to cool completely on a wire rack.

4 To make the butter cream, heat the chocolate and milk gently in a pan until the chocolate has melted, stirring to combine. Leave to cool slightly. Beat together the butter and icing sugar until light and fluffy. Beat in the orange liqueur. Gradually beat in the chocolate mixture.

5 To assemble, cut both cakes into 1-cm/½-inch slices, then reassemble them by sandwiching the slices together with some of the butter cream.

6 Place the 2 reassembled cakes end to end on a serving plate and join them with a little butter cream. Spread the remaining butter cream over the top and sides. Decorate with the chocolate curls, then serve the cake cut diagonally into slices.

SERVES 8

125 g/4½ oz soft margarine
125 g/4½ oz caster sugar
2 eggs
100 g/3½ oz self-raising flour
25 g/1 oz cocoa powder
2 tbsp milk

butter cream
75 g/2¾ oz white chocolate
2 tbsp milk
150 g/5½ oz butter
125 g/4½ oz icing sugar
2 tbsp orange-flavoured liqueur
Quick Chocolate Curls (see page 15), to decorate

moderate
55 mins
40 mins

A dark chocolate sponge sandwiched together with a light creamy orange mousse, this spectacular cake is irresistible.

Mousse Cake

SERVES 12

175 g/6 oz butter
175 g/6 oz caster sugar
4 eggs, beaten lightly
200 g/7 oz self-raising flour
1 tbsp cocoa powder
50 g/1¾ oz dark, orange-flavoured chocolate, melted

orange mousse

2 eggs, separated
4 tbsp caster sugar
200 ml/7 fl oz freshly squeezed orange juice
2 tsp gelatine
3 tbsp water
300 ml/10 fl oz double cream
peeled orange slices, to decorate

1 Grease a 20-cm/8-inch springform cake tin and and line the base with baking paper. Beat the butter and sugar in a bowl until light and fluffy. Gradually add the eggs, beating well after each addition. Sift together the flour and cocoa and fold into the cake mixture. Fold in the chocolate.

2 Pour into the prepared tin and level the top. Bake in a preheated oven, 180°C/350°F/Gas Mark 4, for 40 minutes or until springy to the touch. Leave to cool for 5 minutes in the tin, then turn out and leave to cool completely on a wire rack.

3 To make the orange mousse, beat the egg yolks and sugar until light, then whisk in the orange juice. Sprinkle the gelatine over the water in a small bowl and allow to go spongy, then place over a pan of hot water and stir until dissolved. Stir into the mousse.

4 Whip the cream until holding its shape, reserve a little for decoration and fold the rest into the mousse. Using a clean whisk, whisk the egg whites until standing in soft peaks, then fold in. Leave in a cool place until starting to set, stirring occasionally.

5 Cut the cold cake horizontally into 2 layers. Place one layer of the cake in the tin. Pour in the mousse and press the second cake layer on top. Chill until set. Transfer to a dish, pipe cream rosettes on the top and arrange orange slices in the centre.

moderate

1 hr 15 mins

40 mins

Don't worry if the cake cracks when rolled – this is quite normal. If it doesn't crack, consider yourself a real chocolate wizard in the kitchen!

Chocolate Roulade

1 Line a 38 x 25-cm/15 x 10-inch Swiss roll tin with baking paper. Melt the chocolate in the water, stirring. Leave to cool slightly.

2 Place the eggs and sugar in a bowl and whisk for 10 minutes or until the mixture is pale and foamy and the whisk leaves a trail when lifted. Whisk in the chocolate in a thin stream. Sift the flour and cocoa together and fold into the mixture. Pour into the tin and level the top.

3 Bake in a preheated oven, 200°C/ 400°F/Gas Mark 6, for 12 minutes. Dust a sheet of baking paper with a little icing sugar, turn out the roulade on to it and peel off the lining paper. Roll up the roulade with the fresh paper inside. Place on a wire rack, cover with a damp tea towel and leave to cool.

4 Whisk the cream. Unroll the roulade and spread with the cream. Scatter over the sliced strawberries and re-roll.

5 Place the roulade on a plate and dust it with icing sugar. Serve sliced, decorated with chocolate leaves and strawberries.

SERVES 6
150 g/5½ oz dark chocolate
2 tbsp water
6 eggs
175 g/6 oz caster sugar
3 tbsp plain flour
1 tbsp cocoa powder
icing sugar, to dust

filling
300 ml/10 fl oz double cream
75 g/2¾ oz sliced strawberries

to decorate
icing sugar
chocolate Leaves (see page 15)
strawberries

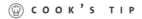 **COOK'S TIP**

Try adding chopped stem ginger to the cream filling instead of strawberries.

 moderate
1 hr
12 mins

This cake originates from Hungary and consists of thin layers of light sponge sandwiched with butter cream and topped with crunchy caramel.

Dobos Torte

SERVES 8

3 eggs
100 g/3½ oz caster sugar
1 tsp vanilla essence
100 g/3½ oz plain flour, sifted

filling
175 g/6 oz dark chocolate
175 g/6 oz butter
2 tbsp milk
350 g/12 oz icing sugar, sifted

caramel
100 g/3½ oz granulated sugar
4 tbsp water

1 Draw four 18-cm/7-inch circles on sheets of baking paper and cut them out. Take 2 baking trays and place a circle upside down on each.

2 Whisk the eggs and caster sugar in a large mixing bowl with an electric whisk for 10 minutes or until the mixture is light and foamy and the whisk leaves a trail. Fold in the vanilla essence and flour, using a metal spoon.

3 Spoon a quarter of the mixture on to one of the paper circles and spread out to the size of the circle. Repeat with the other circle. Bake in a preheated oven, 200°C/400°F/Gas Mark 6, for 5–8 minutes or until golden brown. Transfer to wire racks to cool. Repeat with the remaining mixture.

4 To make the filling, melt the chocolate and cool slightly. Beat the butter, milk and icing sugar until pale and fluffy. Whisk in the chocolate.

5 Place the sugar and water for the caramel in a heavy-based pan. Heat gently, stirring, to dissolve the sugar. Boil gently until pale golden in colour. Remove from the heat. Pour over one cake layer as a topping. Leave to harden slightly. Mark out 8 portions with an oiled knife.

6 Remove the cakes from the paper and trim the edges. Sandwich the layers together with some of the filling, finishing with the caramel-topped cake. Place on a serving plate, spread the sides with the remaining filling mixture and pipe 8 rosettes around the top.

challenging

40 mins

10–16 mins

This rich melt-in-the-mouth cake originates in Austria. Writing the name on top requires a steady hand – drizzle a random scribble if you prefer.

Sachertorte

1 Grease a 23-cm/9-inch springform cake tin and line the base with baking paper. Beat the butter and 75 g/2¾ oz of the sugar until pale and fluffy. Add the egg yolks and beat together well. Add the chocolate in a thin stream, beating well. Fold in the flour. Whisk the egg whites until they stand in soft peaks. Add the remaining sugar and whisk for 2 minutes by hand, or 45–60 seconds if using an electric whisk, until glossy. Fold half into the chocolate mixture, then fold in the remainder.

2 Spoon into the prepared tin and level the top. Bake in a preheated oven, 150°C/300°F/Gas Mark 2, for 1–1¼ hours, until a skewer inserted into the centre comes out clean. Cool in the tin for 5 minutes, then transfer to a wire rack to cool completely.

3 To make the icing, melt the chocolate and beat in the coffee until smooth. Sift the icing sugar into a bowl. Whisk in the melted chocolate mixture to give a thick icing. Cut the cake into 2 layers. Warm the jam, spread over one half of the cake and sandwich together. Invert the cake on a wire rack. Spoon the icing over the cake and spread to coat the top and sides. Leave to set for 5 minutes, allowing any excess icing to drop through the rack. Transfer to a serving plate and leave to set for at least 2 hours.

4 To decorate, spoon the melted chocolate into a small piping bag and pipe the word 'Sacher' or 'Sachertorte' across the top of the cake. Leave to harden before serving the cake.

SERVES 10
150 g/5½ oz unsalted butter
150 g/5½ oz caster sugar
6 eggs, separated
175 g/6 oz dark chocolate, melted
150 g/5½ oz plain flour, sifted

icing and filling
175 g/6 oz dark chocolate
5 tbsp strong black coffee
175 g/6 oz icing sugar
6 tbsp good apricot preserve
50 g/1¾ oz dark chocolate, melted

★★★★ challenging
🕐 3 hrs 30 mins
🕐 1 hr–1 hr 15 mins

Ganache – a divine mixture of chocolate and cream – is used to fill and decorate this rich chocolate cake, making it a chocolate-lover's dream.

Chocolate Ganache Cake

SERVES 10

175 g/6 oz butter
175 g/6 oz caster sugar
4 eggs, beaten lightly
200 g/7 oz self-raising flour
1 tbsp cocoa powder
50 g/1¾ oz dark chocolate, melted

ganache
450ml/16 fl oz double cream
375 g/13 oz dark chocolate, broken
  into pieces

to finish
200 g/7 oz chocolate-flavoured
  cake covering

1 Lightly grease a 20-cm/8-inch springform cake tin and line the base. Beat the butter and sugar until light and fluffy. Gradually add the eggs, beating well after each addition. Sift together the flour and cocoa. Fold into the cake mixture. Fold in the melted chocolate.

2 Pour into the prepared tin and level the top. Bake in a preheated oven, 180°C/350°F/Gas Mark 4, for 40 minutes or until springy to the touch. Leave to cool for 5 minutes in the tin, then turn out on to a wire rack and leave to cool completely. Cut the cold cake into 2 layers.

3 To make the ganache, place the double cream in a pan and bring to the boil, stirring. Add the chocolate and stir until melted and combined. Pour into a bowl and whisk for about 5 minutes or until the ganache is fluffy and cool.

4 Reserve one third of the ganache. Use the remaining ganache to sandwich the cake together and to spread over the top and sides of the cake.

5 Melt the chocolate-flavoured cake covering and spread it over a large sheet of baking paper. Cool until just set. Cut into strips a little wider than the height of the cake. Place the strips around the sides of the cake, overlapping them slightly.

6 Pipe the reserved ganache in tear drops or shells to cover the top of the cake. Chill for 1 hour.

✪✪✪✪ challenging
2 hrs 5 mins
40 mins

This is the traditional French Christmas cake. It consists of a chocolate Swiss roll filled with and encased in a delicious rich chocolate icing.

Bûche *de* Noël

1 Grease and line a 30 x 23-cm/ 12 x 9-inch Swiss roll tin.

2 Whisk the eggs and caster sugar in a bowl with an electric whisk for 10 minutes or until the mixture is light and foamy and the whisk leaves a trail. Sift the flour and cocoa powder and fold in. Pour into the tin and bake in a preheated oven, 200°C/400°F/Gas Mark 6, for 12 minutes or until springy to the touch. Turn out on to baking paper sprinkled with caster sugar. Peel off the lining paper and trim the edges. Cut a small slit halfway into the cake, about 1 cm/½ inch from one short end. Starting at that end, roll up, enclosing the paper. Cool on a wire rack.

3 To make the icing, break the chocolate into pieces and melt over a pan of hot water. Beat in the egg yolks, whisk in the milk and cook, stirring, until the mixture thickens enough to coat the back of a wooden spoon. Cover with dampened greaseproof paper and cool. Beat the butter and sugar until pale and fluffy. Beat in the cooled chocolate custard and the rum, if using.

4 Unroll the sponge, spread with one third of the icing and roll up again. Place on a serving plate. Spread the remaining icing over the cake and mark with a fork to give the effect of tree bark. Leave to set. Pipe white icing at the ends to form the rings of the log. Sprinkle with icing sugar and decorate with holly leaves.

SERVES 10

cake
4 eggs
100 g/3½ oz caster sugar, plus sugar
    for dusting
75 g/2¾ oz self-raising flour
2 tbsp cocoa powder

icing
150 g/5½ oz dark chocolate
2 egg yolks
150 ml/5 fl oz milk
125 g/4½ oz butter
4 tbsp icing sugar
2 tbsp rum (optional)

to decorate
a little white glacé or royal icing
icing sugar, to dust
holly leaves

★★★★ challenging

 1 hr

12 mins

Soft chocolate sponge
topped with a rich
chocolate truffle mixture
makes a cake that
chocoholics will die for.

Chocolate Truffle Cake

SERVES 12

75 g/2¾ oz butter
75 g/2¾ oz caster sugar
2 eggs, beaten lightly
75 g/2¾ oz self-raising flour
½ tsp baking powder
25 g/1 oz cocoa powder
50 g/1¾ oz ground almonds

truffle topping
350 g/12 oz dark chocolate
100 g/3½ oz butter
300 ml/10 fl oz double cream
75 g/2¾ oz plain cake crumbs
3 tbsp dark rum

to decorate
Cape gooseberries
50 g/1¾ oz dark chocolate, melted

1 Lightly grease a 20-cm/8-inch round springform tin and line the base. Beat together the butter and sugar until light and fluffy. Gradually add the eggs, beating well after each addition.

2 Sift the flour, baking powder and cocoa powder together and fold into the mixture along with the ground almonds. Pour into the prepared tin and bake in a preheated oven, 180°C/350°F/Gas Mark 4, for 20–25 minutes or until springy to the touch. Leave to cool slightly in the tin, then transfer to a wire rack to cool completely. Wash and dry the tin and return the cooled cake to the tin.

3 To make the topping, heat the chocolate, butter and cream in a heavy-based pan over a low heat and stir until smooth. Cool, then chill for 30 minutes. Beat well with a wooden spoon and chill for a further 30 minutes. Beat the mixture again, then add the cake crumbs and rum, beating until well combined. Spoon over the sponge base and chill for 3 hours.

4 Meanwhile, dip the Cape gooseberries in the melted chocolate until partially covered. Leave to set on baking paper. Transfer the cake to a serving plate and decorate with Cape gooseberries.

✪✪✪　moderate
🕐　4 hrs 45 mins
🕐　20–25 mins

A light white sponge, topped with a rich, creamy-white chocolate truffle mixture, makes an out-of-this-world gâteau.

White Truffle Cake

1 Grease a 20-cm/8-inch round springform tin and line the base.

2 Whisk the eggs and caster sugar in a mixing bowl for 10 minutes or until very light and foamy and the whisk leaves a trail that lasts a few seconds when lifted. Sift the flour and fold in with a metal spoon. Fold in the melted white chocolate. Pour into the tin and bake in a preheated oven, 180°C/350°F/Gas Mark 4, for 25 minutes or until springy to the touch. Leave to cool slightly, then transfer to a wire rack to cool completely. Wash and dry the tin and return the cold cake to it.

3 To make the topping, place the cream in a pan and bring to the boil, stirring to prevent it from sticking to the bottom of the pan. Cool slightly, then add the white chocolate pieces and stir until melted and combined. Remove from the heat and set aside until almost cool, stirring, then stir in the fromage frais. Pour the mixture on top of the cake and chill for 2 hours.

4 Remove the cake from the tin and transfer to a serving plate. Decorate with caraque and dust with cocoa powder.

SERVES 12

2 eggs
4 tbsp caster sugar
5½ tbsp plain flour
50 g/1¾ oz white chocolate, melted

truffle topping
300 ml/10 fl oz double cream
350 g/12 oz white chocolate, broken into pieces
250 g/9 oz fromage frais

to decorate
dark, milk or white chocolate Caraque (see page 15)
cocoa powder, to dust

🍳 **COOK'S TIP**
Strawberries or raspberries would make a delicious alternative topping.

  easy
3 hrs 15 mins
25 mins

A vacherin is made of layers of crisp meringue sandwiched together with fruit and cream. It makes a fabulous gâteau for special occasions.

Raspberry Vacherin

SERVES 10

3 egg whites
175 g/6 oz caster sugar
1 tsp cornflour
25 g/1 oz dark chocolate, grated

filling

175 g/6 oz dark chocolate
475 ml/16 fl oz double cream, whipped
350 g/12 oz fresh raspberries
a little melted chocolate, to decorate

1 Draw 3 rectangles, 10 x 25 cm/4 x 10 inches, on sheets of baking paper and place on 2 baking trays.

2 Whisk the egg whites in a mixing bowl until standing in soft peaks, then gradually whisk in half of the sugar and continue whisking until the mixture is very stiff and glossy. Carefully fold in the rest of the sugar, the cornflour and grated chocolate with a metal spoon or a spatula.

3 Spoon the meringue mixture into a piping bag fitted with a 1-cm/½-inch plain nozzle and pipe lines across the baking paper rectangles.

4 Bake in a preheated oven, 140°C/275°F/Gas Mark 1, for 1½ hours, changing the positions of the baking trays halfway through cooking. Without opening the oven door, turn off the oven and leave the meringues inside it to cool, then peel away the paper.

5 To make the vacherin filling, melt the chocolate and spread it over 2 of the meringue layers. Leave to stand until the chocolate has set.

6 Place 1 chocolate-coated meringue on a plate and top with about one third of the cream and raspberries. Gently place the second chocolate-coated meringue on top and spread with half of the remaining cream and raspberries.

7 Place the last meringue on the top and decorate it with the remaining cream and raspberries. Drizzle a little melted chocolate over the top.

★★★★ challenging

1 hr 45 mins

1 hr 30 mins

The addition of nuts and raisins has given this dessert extra texture, making it similar to that of chocolate brownies.

Chocolate Brownie Roulade

1 Grease a 30 x 20-cm/12 x 8-inch Swiss roll tin, line with baking paper and grease the paper.

2 Place the chocolate with the water in a small saucepan over a low heat, stirring until the chocolate has just melted. Leave to cool.

3 In a bowl, whisk the sugar and egg yolks for 2–3 minutes with an electric whisk until thick and pale. Fold in the cooled chocolate, the raisins and the pecan nuts.

4 In a separate bowl, whisk the egg whites with the salt. Fold one quarter of the egg whites into the chocolate mixture, then fold in the rest of the whites, working lightly and quickly.

5 Transfer the mixture to the prepared tin and bake in a preheated oven, 180°C/350°F/Gas Mark 4, for 25 minutes, until risen and just firm to the touch. Leave to cool slightly, cover with a sheet of non-stick baking paper and a damp clean tea towel and leave to stand until completely cold.

6 Turn the roulade out on to another piece of baking paper dusted with icing sugar and peel off the lining paper.

7 Trim the edges of the roulade and spread with the cream. Starting from a short end, roll the sponge away from you, using the paper to guide you. Transfer to a serving plate and chill until ready to serve. Dust thickly with icing sugar before serving.

SERVES 8

150 g/5 ½ oz dark chocolate, broken into pieces
3 tbsp water
175 g/6 oz caster sugar
5 eggs, separated
25 g/1 oz raisins, chopped
25 g/1 oz pecan nuts, chopped
pinch of salt
300 ml/10 fl oz double cream, whipped lightly
icing sugar, to dust

★★★ moderate

1 hr

25 mins

The white chocolate makes this a very rich cake, so it is best to serve it cut into small squares or bars, or sliced thinly.

Chocolate *and* Apricot Squares

SERVES 12

125 g/4½ oz butter
175 g/6 oz white chocolate, chopped
4 eggs
125 g/4½ oz caster sugar
200 g/7 oz plain flour, sifted
1 tsp baking powder
pinch of salt
100 g/3½ oz ready-to-eat dried apricots, chopped

1 Lightly grease a 23-cm/9-inch square cake tin and line the base with a sheet of baking paper.

2 Melt the butter and chocolate in a heatproof bowl set over a saucepan of simmering water. Stir frequently with a wooden spoon until the mixture is smooth and glossy. Leave the mixture to cool slightly.

3 Beat the eggs and caster sugar into the butter and chocolate mixture until well combined.

4 Fold in the flour, baking powder, salt and chopped dried apricots and mix together well.

5 Pour the mixture into the tin and bake in a preheated oven, 180°C/350°F/Gas Mark 4, for 25–30 minutes. The centre of the cake may not be completely firm, but it will set as it cools. Leave in the tin to cool.

6 When the cake is completely cold turn it out and slice into squares or bars.

🍳 **COOK'S TIP**

Replace the white chocolate with milk or dark chocolate, if you prefer.

⭐⭐ easy
🕐 50 mins
🕐 25–30 mins

Serve this tasty snack plain, with butter or jam or, Italian style, with mascarpone cheese.

Italian Chocolate Chip Bread

1 Oil a baking tray. Sift the flour, cocoa powder and salt into a bowl. Add the butter, cut it into the flour mixture, then stir in the sugar and yeast.

2 Gradually add the water to the mixture, stirring well to combine. When the dough becomes too firm to stir with a spoon, gather it together with your hands. Turn it out on to a lightly floured surface and knead thoroughly until smooth and elastic.

3 Knead the chocolate chips into the dough, distributing them evenly throughout. Form the dough into a round loaf, place the loaf on the baking tray, cover with oiled clingfilm and set aside in a warm place for 1½–2 hours, until doubled in bulk.

4 Remove and discard the clingfilm and bake the loaf in a preheated oven, 220°C/425°F/Gas Mark 7, for 10 minutes. Lower the temperature to 190°C/375°F/Gas Mark 5 and bake for a further 15 minutes.

5 Transfer the loaf to a wire rack and brush with melted butter. Cover with a clean tea towel until cooled.

SERVES 4

225 g/8 oz plain flour, plus flour for dusting
1 tbsp cocoa powder
pinch of salt
1 tbsp unsalted butter, plus ½ tsp extra, melted, for brushing
1 tbsp caster sugar
1 tsp easy-blend dried yeast
150 ml/5 fl oz hand-hot water
55 g/2 oz dark chocolate chips

easy

2 hrs 30 mins

25 mins

The sweetness of the whipped marshmallow frosting complements the mouthwatering flavour of this moist, dark chocolate sponge cake.

Chocolate Marshmallow Cake

SERVES 6

6 tbsp unsalted butter
225 g/8 oz caster sugar
1/2 tsp vanilla essence
2 eggs, beaten lightly
85 g/3 oz dark chocolate, broken into pieces
150 ml/5 fl oz buttermilk
175 g/6 oz self-raising flour
1/2 tsp bicarbonate of soda
pinch of salt
55 g/2 oz milk chocolate, grated, to decorate

frosting
175 g/6 oz white marshmallows
1 tbsp milk
2 egg whites
2 tbsp caster sugar

1 Grease an 850-ml/1½-pint ovenproof pudding basin. Cream the butter, caster sugar and vanilla essence together until very pale and fluffy, then gradually beat in the eggs.

2 Melt the dark chocolate in a heatproof bowl over a pan of simmering water. When the chocolate has melted, gradually stir in the buttermilk, until well combined. Remove the pan from the heat and cool slightly.

3 Sift the flour, bicarbonate of soda and salt into a separate bowl.

4 Alternately add the chocolate mixture and the flour to the creamed mixture, a little at a time. Spoon into the basin and smooth the surface.

5 Bake in a preheated oven, 160°C/325°F/Gas Mark 3, for about 50 minutes, until a skewer inserted into the centre of the cake comes out clean. Turn out on to a wire rack to cool.

6 Meanwhile, make the frosting. Put the marshmallows and milk in a small saucepan and heat very gently until the marshmallows have melted. Remove the pan from the heat and leave to cool.

7 Whisk the egg whites until soft peaks form, then add the sugar and continue whisking until stiff peaks form. Fold the egg white into the cooled marshmallow mixture and set aside for 10 minutes.

8 When the cake is cool, cover the top and sides with the marshmallow frosting. Sprinkle grated milk chocolate over the frosting.

moderate

1 hr 30 mins

55 mins

Ideal for children to make, this cake does not require an oven and it is prepared very rapidly – but it does need to chill overnight.

No-bake Refrigerator Cake

1 Line a 450 g/1-lb loaf tin with greaseproof paper or baking paper.

2 Put the butter and chocolate in the top of a double boiler or in a heatproof bowl set over a pan of barely simmering water. Stir constantly over a low heat until they have melted and the mixture is smooth. Remove from the heat and leave to cool slightly.

3 In a separate bowl, mix together the cherries and walnuts. Spoon one-third of the chocolate mixture into the prepared tin, cover with a layer of biscuits and top with half the cherries and walnuts. Make further layers, ending with a layer of chocolate mixture. Cover with clingfilm and chill in the refrigerator for at least 12 hours. Turn the cake on to a serving dish and cut into thin slices.

SERVES 6

225 g/8 oz unsalted butter, diced
225 g/8 oz dark chocolate, broken into pieces
55 g/2 oz glacé cherries, chopped
55 g/2 oz walnuts, chopped
12 rectangular plain chocolate biscuits

 COOK'S TIP

Try replacing the cherries and walnuts with chopped dried apricots and almonds, or raisins and pecan nuts.

easy
12 hrs 20 mins
5–8 mins

This is the ideal snack to eat with a mid-morning cup of coffee. Serve with whipped cream for a special treat.

Swedish Chocolate Cake

SERVES 6–8

25 g/1 oz dry white breadcrumbs
5 tbsp unsalted butter
175 g/6 oz caster sugar
2 eggs, separated
1 tsp vanilla essence
175 g/6 oz plain flour
1 tsp baking powder
125 ml/4 fl oz single cream
85 g/3 oz dark chocolate, melted

1 Grease a deep 23-cm/9-inch round cake tin. Sprinkle the breadcrumbs into the tin and press them on to the base and sides.

2 Cream the butter with the sugar until pale and fluffy. Beat in the egg yolks, one at a time, and add the vanilla.

3 Sift one third of the flour with the baking powder, then beat into the egg mixture. Mix together the cream and melted chocolate, then beat one-third of this mixture into the egg mixture. Continue adding the flour and the chocolate mixture alternately, beating well after each addition.

4 Whisk the egg whites in a separate bowl until they form stiff peaks. Fold the egg whites into the chocolate mixture.

5 Pour into the prepared tin and bake in a preheated oven, 150°C/300°F/Gas Mark 2, for about 50 minutes, until a skewer inserted into the centre of the cake comes out clean. Turn the cake out on to a wire rack to cool completely before serving in slices.

★★★ moderate

30 mins

1 hr

🍳 COOK'S TIP

Try flavouring this cake with the grated rind of half an orange instead of the vanilla essence.

Moist and moreish, this fruity chocolate cake will prove to be a popular after-school snack.

Date *and* Chocolate Cake

1 Grease and flour two 18-cm/7-inch sandwich tins. Put the chocolate, grenadine and syrup in the top of a double boiler or in a heatproof bowl set over a pan of barely simmering water. Stir over a low heat until the chocolate has melted and the mixture is smooth. Remove from the heat and leave to cool.

2 Cream the butter and caster sugar together until pale and fluffy, then gradually heat in the eggs and then the cooled chocolate mixture.

3 Sift the flour into another bowl and stir in the ground rice. Fold the flour mixture into the creamed mixture.

4 Divide the mixture between the prepared tins and smooth the surface. Bake in a preheated oven, 180°C/350°F/ Gas Mark 4, for 20–25 minutes, until golden and firm to the touch. Turn out on to a wire rack to cool completely.

5 To make the filling, put all the ingredients into a saucepan and stir over a low heat for 4–5 minutes, until thoroughly combined. Remove from the heat, leave to cool and then use the filling to sandwich the cakes together. Dust the top of the cake with icing sugar to decorate.

SERVES 4

115 g/4 oz dark chocolate, broken into pieces
1 tbsp grenadine
1 tbsp golden syrup
115 g/4 oz unsalted butter
55 g/2 oz caster sugar
2 large eggs
85 g/3 oz self-raising flour
2 tbsp ground rice
1 tbsp icing sugar, to decorate

FILLING

115 g/4 oz dried dates, chopped
1 tbsp lemon juice
1 tbsp orange juice
1 tbsp demerara sugar
25 g/1 oz blanched almonds, chopped
2 tbsp apricot jam

 moderate

25 mins

40 mins

Hot Desserts

Chocolate is comforting at any time but never more so than when served in a steaming hot pudding. It is hard to think of anything more warming, comforting and homely than tucking into a steamed hot Chocolate Fudge Pudding or a Hot Chocolate Soufflé, and children will love the chocolate addition to nursery favourites such as Bread & Butter Pudding. In fact, there are several old favourites that have been given the chocolate treatment, bringing them bang up to date and putting them on the chocolate lover's map.

When you are feeling in need of something a little more sophisticated, try the new-style chocolate Apple Pancake Stacks, or Chocolate Meringue Pie, or Chocolate Zabaglione for a sophisticated, frothy, warm dessert set to get your tastebuds in a whirl! This chapter is packed full of chocolate delights, with different tastes and textures to add warmth to any day.

An old time favourite with an up-to-date twist, this pudding makes the perfect end to a special family meal.

Chocolate Queen *of* Puddings

SERVES 4

50 g/1¾ oz dark chocolate
475 ml/16 fl oz chocolate-flavoured milk
100 g/3½ oz fresh white or
    wholemeal breadcrumbs
125 g/4½ oz caster sugar
2 eggs, separated
4 tbsp black cherry jam

1 Break the chocolate into small pieces and place in a saucepan with the chocolate-flavoured milk. Heat gently, stirring until the chocolate melts. Bring almost to the boil, then remove the pan from the heat.

2 Place the breadcrumbs in a large mixing bowl with 25 g/1 oz of the sugar. Pour over the chocolate milk and mix well. Beat in the egg yolks.

3 Spoon into a 1.25-litre/2-pint pie dish and bake in a preheated oven, 180°C/350°F/Gas Mark 4, for 25–30 minutes or until set and firm.

4 Whisk the egg whites in a large grease-free bowl until standing in soft peaks. Gradually whisk in the remaining caster sugar and whisk until you have a glossy, thick meringue.

5 Spread the black cherry jam over the chocolate base and pile or pipe the meringue on top. Return the pudding to the oven for about 15 minutes or until the meringue is crisp and golden.

⊕ **COOK'S TIP**

If you prefer, add 40 g/1½ oz desiccated coconut to the breadcrumbs and omit the black cherry jam.

★★★   moderate
       25 mins
       40–45 mins

Eve's Pudding is traditionally made with apples and plain sponge, but here raspberries are added, and the fruit is topped with white chocolate sponge.

Chocolate Eve's Pudding

1 Place the apples and raspberries in a shallow 1¼-litre/2-pint ovenproof dish.

2 Place the raspberry jam and port (if using) in a small pan and heat gently, stirring, until the jam melts. Pour the mixture over the fruit.

3 Place all of the ingredients for the sponge topping in a large mixing bowl and beat until the mixture is smooth.

4 Spoon the sponge mixture over the fruit and level the top. Bake in a preheated oven, 180°C/350°F/Gas Mark 4, for 40–45 minutes or until the sponge is springy to the touch.

5 To make the sauce, break the chocolate into small pieces and place in a heavy-based saucepan with the cream. Heat gently, beating until smooth Serve warm with the pudding.

SERVES 4

2 eating apples, peeled, cored and
    sliced thickly
225 g/8 oz fresh or frozen raspberries
4 tbsp seedless raspberry jam
2 tbsp port (optional)

sponge topping
4 tbsp soft margarine
4 tbsp caster sugar
75 g/2¾ oz self-raising flour, sifted
50 g/1¾ oz white chocolate, grated
1 egg
2 tbsp milk

bitter chocolate sauce
90 g/3 oz dark chocolate
150 ml/5 fl oz single cream

 COOK'S TIP

Try using dark chocolate in the sponge, and apricot halves, covered with peach schnapps and apricot conserve, for the base.

easy

15 mins

40–45 mins

Individual puddings always look more professional and are quicker to cook. If you do not have mini pudding basins, you could use small teacups instead.

Chocolate Ginger Puddings

SERVES 4

100 g/3½ oz soft margarine
100 g/3½ oz self-raising flour, sifted
100 g/3½ oz caster sugar
2 eggs
25 g/1 oz cocoa powder, sifted
25 g/1 oz dark chocolate
50 g/1¾ oz stem ginger, plus extra to decorate
icing sugar, to dust

chocolate custard
2 egg yolks
1 tbsp caster sugar
1 tbsp cornflour
300 ml/10 fl oz milk
100 g/3½ oz dark chocolate, broken into pieces

1 Lightly grease 4 individual pudding basins. Place the margarine, flour, sugar, eggs and cocoa powder in a mixing bowl and beat until well combined and smooth. Chop the chocolate and ginger and stir into the mixture.

2 Spoon the mixture into the prepared basins and level the tops. The mixture should three-quarters fill the basins. Cover the puddings with discs of baking paper, then with pleated pieces of foil. Steam for 45 minutes, until the puddings are cooked and springy to the touch.

3 Meanwhile, make the custard. Beat together the egg yolks, sugar and cornflour to form a smooth paste. Heat the milk until boiling and pour over the egg mixture. Return to the pan and cook over a very low heat, stirring, until thick. Remove from the heat, add the chocolate and stir until the chocolate melts.

4 Lift the puddings from the steamer, run a knife around the edges of the basins and turn out on to serving plates. Dust with sugar and drizzle some chocolate custard over the top. Decorate with extra stem ginger. Serve the remaining custard separately.

moderate

10 mins

45 mins

Buttery brioche gives this pudding a lovely rich flavour, but this recipe also works well with soft-baked batch bread.

Bread *and* Butter Pudding

1 Cut the brioche into thin slices. Lightly butter one side of each slice.

2 Place a layer of brioche, buttered side down, in the bottom of a shallow ovenproof dish. Sprinkle a few chocolate chips over the top.

3 Continue layering the brioche and chocolate chips, finishing with a layer of bread on top.

4 Whisk together the egg, egg yolks and sugar until well combined. Heat the milk in a small saucepan until it just begins to simmer. Gradually add to the egg mixture, whisking well.

5 Pour the custard over the pudding and leave to stand for 5 minutes. Press the brioche down into the milk.

6 Place the pudding dish in a roasting tin and add boiling water to come halfway up the side of the dish (this is known as a bain-marie). Bake in a preheated oven, 180°C/350°F/Gas Mark 4, for 30 minutes or until the custard has set. Leave the pudding to cool for 5 minutes before serving.

SERVES 4

225 g/8 oz brioche
1 tbsp butter
50 g/1¾ oz dark chocolate chips
1 egg
2 egg yolks
4 tbsp caster sugar
425 ml/15 fl oz canned light evaporated milk

🍳 COOK'S TIP

For a double-chocolate pudding, heat the milk with 1 tablespoon cocoa powder, stirring until well dissolved, then continue from Step 4.

⭐⭐ easy
🕐 2 hrs 15 mins
🕐 35 mins

This fabulous steamed pudding, served with a rich chocolate fudge sauce, is a warm and welcoming treat on cold winter days.

Chocolate Fudge Pudding

SERVES 6

150 g/5½ oz soft margarine
150 g/5½ oz self-raising flour, sifted
150 g/5½ oz golden syrup
3 eggs
25 g/1 oz cocoa powder

chocolate fudge sauce
100 g/3½ oz dark chocolate
125 ml/4 fl oz condensed milk
4 tbsp double cream

1 Lightly grease a 1.2-litre/2-pint pudding basin.

2 Place all the pudding ingredients in a mixing bowl and beat until well combined and smooth.

3 Spoon into the prepared basin and level the top. Cover with a disc of baking parchment and tie a pleated sheet of foil over the basin. Steam for 1½–2 hours, until the pudding is cooked and springy to the touch.

4 To make the sauce, break the chocolate into small pieces and place in a small pan with the condensed milk. Heat gently, stirring until the chocolate melts. Remove the pan from the heat and stir in the double cream.

5 To serve the pudding, turn it out on to a serving plate and pour over a little of the chocolate fudge sauce. Serve the remaining sauce separately.

★★ easy
🕐 10 mins
🕐 2 hrs

COOK'S TIP

When covering steamed puddings, tie the foil tightly with a length of string, then make a 'handle' with an additional length of string, so that it is easy to lift the basin out of the pan or steamer.

The addition of chocolate in a crumble topping makes it even more of a treat, and is a good way of enticing children to eat a fruit dessert.

Chocolate Fruit Crumble

1 Lightly grease an ovenproof dish with a little butter or margarine.

2 Drain the apricots, reserving 4 tablespoons of the juice. Place the apples and apricots in the prepared ovenproof dish with the reserved apricot juice and toss to mix.

3 Sift the flour into a mixing bowl. Cut the butter into small cubes and rub in with your fingertips until the mixture resembles fine breadcrumbs. Stir in the rolled oats, caster sugar and chocolate chips.

4 Sprinkle the crumble mixture over the apples and apricots and level the top roughly. Do not press the crumble down on to the fruit.

5 Bake in a preheated oven, 180°C/350°F/Gas Mark 4, for 40–45 minutes or until the topping is golden. Serve the crumble hot or cold.

SERVES 4

400 g/14 oz canned apricots in natural juice
450 g/1 lb cooking apples, peeled and
    sliced thickly
100 g/3½ oz plain flour
6 tbsp butter
50 g/1¾ oz rolled oats
4 tbsp caster sugar
100 g/3½ oz chocolate chips

COOK'S TIP

Other fruits can be used to make this crumble – fresh pears mixed with fresh or frozen raspberries work well. If you use fresh fruit, add 4 tablespoon orange juice to the fresh fruit.

easy

5–10 mins

40–45 mins

In this recipe, the mixture separates out during cooking to produce a cream sponge topping and a delicious chocolate sauce on the bottom.

Saucy Chocolate Pudding

SERVES 4

300 ml/10 fl oz milk
75 g/2¾ oz dark chocolate, broken into pieces
½ tsp vanilla essence
100 g/3½ oz caster sugar
100 g/3½ oz butter
150 g/5½ oz self-raising flour
2 tbsp cocoa powder
icing sugar, to dust

for the sauce
3 tbsp cocoa powder
4 tbsp light muscovado sugar
300 ml/10 fl oz boiling water

1 Lightly grease a 900-ml/1½-pint ovenproof dish.

2 Place the milk in a small pan with the chocolate and stir over a gentle heat until the chocolate melts. Leave to cool slightly. Stir in the vanilla essence.

3 Beat together the caster sugar and butter in a bowl until light and fluffy. Sift the flour and cocoa powder together. Add to the bowl with the chocolate milk and beat until smooth, using an electric whisk if you have one. Pour the mixture into the prepared dish.

4 To make the sauce, mix together the cocoa powder and sugar. Add a little of the boiling water and mix to a smooth paste, then stir in the remaining water. Pour the sauce over the pudding mixture but do not mix in.

5 Place the dish on a baking tray and bake in a preheated oven, 180°C/ 350°F/Gas Mark 4, for 40 minutes or until the pudding is dry on top and springy to the touch. Leave to stand for about 5 minutes, then dust with a little icing sugar just before serving.

 COOK'S TIP

For a mocha sauce, add 1 tablespoon instant coffee to the cocoa powder and sugar in Step 4, before mixing to a paste with the boiling water.

easy

15 mins

45 mins

Crumbly biscuit base, rich creamy chocolate filling topped with fluffy meringue – what could be more indulgent than this fabulous dessert?

Chocolate Meringue Pie

1 Place the digestive biscuits in a plastic bag and crush with a rolling pin. Pour into a mixing bowl. Melt the butter and stir it into the biscuit crumbs until well mixed. Press the biscuit mixture firmly into the base and up the sides of a 23-cm/9-inch flan tin or dish.

2 To make the filling, beat the egg yolks, caster sugar and cornflour in a large bowl until they form a smooth paste, adding a little of the milk if necessary. Heat the milk until almost boiling, then slowly pour it on to the egg mixture, whisking well.

3 Return the mixture to the saucepan and cook gently, whisking constantly, until it thickens. Remove from the heat. Whisk in the melted chocolate, then pour it in to the digestive biscuit base.

4 To make the meringue, whisk the egg whites in a large mixing bowl until standing in soft peaks. Gradually whisk in about two thirds of the sugar until the mixture is stiff and glossy. Fold in the remaining sugar and the vanilla essence.

5 Spread the meringue over the filling, swirling the surface with the back of a spoon to give it an attractive finish. Bake in the centre of a preheated oven, 160°C/325°F/Gas Mark 3, for 30 minutes or until golden. Serve hot or just warm.

SERVES 6

225 g/8 oz dark chocolate digestive biscuits
4 tbsp butter

filling
3 egg yolks
4 tbsp caster sugar
4 tbsp cornflour
600 ml/1 pint milk
100 g/3½ oz dark chocolate, melted

meringue
2 egg whites
100 g/3¼ oz caster sugar
¼ tsp vanilla essence

✪✪✪✪ challenging
🕐 30 mins
🕐 35 mins

Pancakes are given the chocolate treatment here to make a fabulous dinner party dessert. Prepare them ahead of time for trouble-free entertaining.

Chocolate *and* Banana Pancakes

SERVES 4

3 large bananas
6 tbsp orange juice
grated rind of 1 orange
2 tbsp orange- or banana-flavoured liqueur

hot chocolate sauce

1 tbsp cocoa powder
2 tsp cornflour
3 tbsp milk
40 g/1½ oz dark chocolate
1 tbsp butter
175 g/6 oz golden syrup
¼ tsp vanilla essence

pancakes

100 g/3½ oz plain flour
1 tbsp cocoa powder
1 egg
1 tsp sunflower oil
300 ml/10 fl oz milk
oil, for frying

1 Peel and slice the bananas and place them in a dish with the orange juice and rind and the liqueur.

2 Mix the cocoa powder and cornflour in a bowl, then stir in the milk. Break the dark chocolate into pieces and place in a pan with the butter and golden syrup. Heat gently, stirring until well blended. Add the cocoa mixture and bring to the boil over a gentle heat, stirring. Simmer for 1 minute, then remove from the heat and stir in the vanilla essence.

3 To make the pancakes, sift the flour and cocoa into a mixing bowl and make a well in the centre. Add the egg and oil. Gradually whisk in the milk to form a smooth batter. Heat a little oil in a heavy-based frying pan and pour off any excess. Pour in a little batter and tilt the pan to coat the base. Cook over a medium heat until the underside is browned. Flip over and cook the other side. Slide the pancake out of the pan and keep warm. Repeat until all the batter has been used.

4 To serve, reheat the chocolate sauce. Fold the pancakes into quarters and fill with the banana slices. Pour over a little chocolate sauce and serve.

✪✪✪✪ challenging

🕐 10 mins

🕐 15 mins

If you cannot wait to get your first chocolate 'fix' of the day, serve these pancakes for breakfast. They also make a perfect family dessert.

Apple Pancake Stacks

1 Sift the flour and baking powder into a mixing bowl. Stir in the caster sugar. Make a well in the centre and add the egg and melted butter. Gradually whisk in the milk to form a smooth batter.

2 Peel, core and grate the apple and stir in with the chocolate chips.

3 Heat a griddle or heavy-based frying pan over a medium heat and grease it lightly. For each pancake, place about 2 tablespoons of the batter on to the griddle or pan and spread to make a 7.5-cm/3-inch round.

4 Cook for a few minutes until you see bubbles appear on the surface of the pancake. Turn over and cook for a further 1 minute. Remove from the pan and keep warm. Repeat with the remaining batter to make about 12 pancakes.

5 To serve, stack 2 or 3 pancakes on an individual serving plate and drizzle with the hot chocolate sauce or maple syrup.

SERVES 4

225 g/8 oz plain flour
1½ tsp baking powder
4 tbsp caster sugar
1 egg
1 tbsp butter, melted, plus butter
    for greasing
300 ml/10 fl oz milk
1 eating apple
50 g/1¾ oz dark chocolate chips
Glossy Chocolate Sauce (see page 75) or
    maple syrup, to serve

🍳 **COOK'S TIP**

To keep the cooked pancakes warm, pile them on top of each other with baking paper in between to prevent them from sticking to one another.

 moderate

⏲ 20 mins

🕐 45 mins

This is a fun dessert to serve at the end of the meal. Prepare in advance, then just warm through before serving.

Chocolate Fondue

SERVES 4

225 g/8 oz dark chocolate
200 ml/7 fl oz double cream
2 tbsp brandy

to serve
selection of fruit
white and pink marshmallows
sweet biscuits

1 Break the chocolate into small pieces and place in a small saucepan with the cream. Heat the mixture gently, stirring constantly until the chocolate has melted and blended with the cream.

2 Remove the pan from the heat and stir in the brandy.

3 Pour into a fondue pot or a small flameproof dish and keep warm, preferably over a small burner.

4 Serve with a selection of fruit, marshmallows and biscuits for dipping. The fruit and marshmallows can be spiked on fondue forks, wooden skewers or ordinary forks for dipping into the chocolate fondue.

⭐ very easy
🕐 15 mins
🕐 5 mins

COOK'S TIP

To prepare the fruit for dipping, cut larger fruit into bite-sized pieces. Fruit that discolours, such as bananas, apples and pears, should be dipped in a little lemon juice as soon as it is cut.

Served with chocolate custard, this wonderful, light soufflé is a chocoholic's dream.

Hot Chocolate Soufflé

1 Grease a 900-ml/1½-pint soufflé dish and sprinkle with caster sugar.

2 Heat the milk with the butter in a pan until almost boiling. Mix the egg yolks, cornflour and caster sugar in a bowl and pour on some of the hot milk, whisking. Return it to the pan and cook gently, stirring constantly until thickened. Break the chocolate into pieces and stir into the mixture until melted. Remove from the heat and stir in the vanilla essence.

3 Whisk the egg whites until standing in soft peaks. Fold half of the egg whites into the chocolate mixture. Fold in the rest with the chocolate chips. Pour into the dish and bake in a preheated oven, 180°C/350°F/Gas Mark 4, for 40–45 minutes, until well risen.

4 Meanwhile, make the custard. Put the cornflour and sugar in a small bowl and mix to a smooth paste with a little of the milk. Heat the remaining milk until almost boiling. Pour a little of the hot milk on to the cornflour, mix well, then pour back into the pan. Cook gently, stirring until thickened. Break the chocolate into pieces and add to the custard, stirring until melted.

5 Dust the soufflé with icing sugar and serve immediately with the chocolate custard.

SERVES **4**

300 ml/10 fl oz milk
2 tbsp butter
4 large eggs, separated
1 tbsp cornflour
4 tbsp caster sugar
100 g/3½ oz dark chocolate
½ tsp vanilla essence
100 g/3½ oz dark chocolate chips
caster and icing sugar, to dust

chocolate custard
2 tbsp cornflour
1 tbsp caster sugar
450 ml/16 fl oz milk
50 g/1¾ oz dark chocolate

★★★★ challenging
🕐 15 mins
🕐 40–45 mins

As this recipe uses only
a little chocolate, choose
one with a minimum of
70 per cent cocoa solids for
a good flavour.

Chocolate Zabaglione

S E R V E S   4

4 egg yolks
4 tbsp caster sugar
50 g/1¾ oz dark chocolate
125 ml/4 fl oz Marsala wine
cocoa powder, to dust

1 In a large glass mixing bowl and using an electric whisk, whisk together the
egg yolks and caster sugar until the mixture is very pale.

2 Grate the chocolate finely and fold into the egg mixture with the Marsala.

3 Place the mixing bowl over a saucepan of gently simmering water and set
the electric whisk on the lowest speed or swap to a balloon whisk. Cook
gently, whisking constantly, until the mixture thickens; take care not to
overcook or the mixture will curdle.

4 Spoon the hot mixture into warmed individual glass dishes or coffee cups
and dust with cocoa powder. Serve the zabaglione as soon as possible, while
it is warm, light and fluffy.

 C O O K ' S   T I P

Make the dessert just before serving as it will separate if left to stand. If it
begins to curdle, remove it from the heat immediately, place it in a bowl of cold
water to stop the cooking and whisk furiously until smooth.

⭐⭐   easy
🕐   10 mins
🕐   5 mins

This sponge pudding is very light and tastes utterly delicious with a coffee or chocolate sauce.

Steamed Coffee Sponge

1 Lightly grease a 600-ml/1-pint pudding basin. Cream the margarine and sugar until light and fluffy and beat in the eggs.

2 Sift the flour and baking powder on to the mixture and stir in. Stir in the milk and coffee essence to make a smooth batter.

3 Spoon the mixture into the pudding basin and cover with a pleated piece of baking paper and then a pleated piece of foil, securing around the bowl with string. Place in a steamer or large pan half full of boiling water. Cover and steam for 1–1¼ hours or until cooked through.

4 To make the sauce, put the milk, soft brown sugar and cocoa in a pan and heat until the sugar dissolves. Blend the cornflour with 4 tablespoons cold water to make a paste and stir into the pan. Bring the sauce to the boil, stirring until thickened. Cook over a gentle heat for 1 minute.

5 Turn the pudding out on to a serving plate and spoon the sauce over the top. Serve at once.

SERVES 4

2 tbsp margarine
2 tbsp soft brown sugar
2 eggs
5½ tbsp plain flour
¾ tsp baking powder
6 tbsp milk
1 tsp coffee essence

sauce
300 ml/10 fl oz milk
1 tbsp soft brown sugar
1 tsp cocoa powder
2 tbsp cornflour

COOK'S TIP

The pudding is covered with pleated paper and foil to allow it to rise. The foil will react with the steam and must therefore not be placed directly against the pudding.

★★★   moderate
🕐   10 mins
🕐   1 hr–1 hr 15 mins

This pudding has a hidden surprise when cooked because it separates to give a rich chocolate sauce at the bottom of the dish.

Fudge Pudding

SERVES 4

4 tbsp margarine
6 tbsp soft light brown sugar
2 eggs, beaten
350 ml/12 fl oz milk
50 g/1¾ oz chopped walnuts
5 tbsp plain flour
2 tbsp cocoa powder
icing sugar and cocoa powder, to dust

1 Lightly grease a 1-litre/1¾-pint ovenproof dish.

2 Cream together the margarine and sugar in a large mixing bowl until fluffy. Beat in the eggs. Gradually stir in the milk and add the walnuts.

3 Sift the flour and cocoa powder into the mixture and fold in gently with a metal spoon, until well mixed.

4 Spoon the pudding mixture into the dish and cook in a preheated oven, 180°C/350°F/Gas Mark 4, for 35–40 minutes or until the sponge is cooked.

5 Dust with icing sugar and cocoa powder and serve.

easy
10 mins
35–45 mins

COOK'S TIP

Add 1–2 tablespoons of brandy or rum to the mixture for a slightly alcoholic pudding, or 1–2 tablespoons of orange juice for a child-friendly version.

These rich individual puddings with cream sauce always look and taste impressive at the end of a meal.

Sticky Chocolate Puddings

1 Lightly grease 6 individual 175-ml/ 6-fl oz pudding basins.

2 In a bowl, cream together the butter and sugar until pale and fluffy. Beat in the eggs a little at a time, beating well after each addition.

3 Sift the flour, salt, and cocoa powder into the creamed mixture and fold in with a metal spoon. Stir in the chopped chocolate until evenly combined.

4 Divide the mixture between the prepared pudding basins. Cover the basins with circles of baking paper and then with pleated squares of foil. Press around the edges to seal.

5 Place the basins in a roasting tin and pour in boiling water to come halfway up the sides of the basins.

6 Bake in a preheated oven, 180°C/350°F/Gas Mark 4, for 50 minutes or until a skewer inserted into the centre comes out clean.

7 Meanwhile, make the sauce. Put the cream, sugar and butter in a pan and gradually bring to the boil, stirring constantly to dissolve the sugar. Simmer gently for 1–2 minutes.

8 To serve, run a knife around the edge of each pudding, then turn out on to serving plates. Serve immediately with the cream sauce.

SERVES 6

125 g/4½ oz butter, softened
150 g/5½ oz soft brown sugar
3 eggs, beaten
125 g/4½ oz self-raising flour
pinch of salt
25 g/1 oz cocoa powder
25 g/1 oz dark chocolate, chopped finely
75 g/2¾ oz white chocolate, chopped finely

sauce
150 ml/5 fl oz double cream
75 g/2¾ oz soft brown sugar
2 tbsp butter

✪✪✪   moderate

🕐   20 mins

🕐   1 hr

This chocolate pudding is served with hot fudge sauce, making it the most delicious way to use up bread that is slightly stale.

Chocolate Bread Pudding

SERVES 4

6 thick slices white bread, crusts removed
450 ml/16 fl oz milk
175 g/6 oz canned evaporated milk
2 tbsp cocoa powder
2 eggs
2 tbsp dark muscovado sugar
1 tsp vanilla essence
icing sugar, to dust

hot fudge sauce

1 tbsp cornflour
150 ml/5 fl oz milk
55 g/2 oz dark chocolate, broken into pieces
1 tbsp cocoa powder
2 tbsp golden syrup
55 g/2 oz butter or margarine
2 tbsp dark muscovado sugar

1 Grease a shallow ovenproof dish. Cut the bread into squares and layer them in the dish.

2 Put the milk, evaporated milk and cocoa powder in a saucepan and heat gently, stirring occasionally, until lukewarm.

3 Whisk together the eggs, sugar and vanilla essence. Add the warm milk mixture and whisk well.

4 Pour into the prepared dish, making sure that all the bread is completely covered. Cover with clingfilm and chill in the refrigerator for 1–2 hours.

5 Bake the pudding in a preheated oven, 180°C/350°F/Gas Mark 4, for about 35–40 minutes, until set. Remove the pudding from the oven and allow to stand for 5 minutes.

6 To make the sauce, mix the cornflour to a smooth paste with a little of the milk, then place in a saucepan with the rest of the milk and the remaining sauce ingredients. Heat gently, stirring constantly, until smooth.

7 Dust the pudding with icing sugar and serve with the hot fudge sauce.

✪✪✪   moderate

2 hrs 15 mins

45 mins

Filo pastry makes these empanadas light and crisp on the outside, while the filling melts into a scrumptious hot banana-chocolate goo.

Banana Empanadas

1 Peel and dice the bananas and place in a bowl. Add the sugar and lemon juice and stir well to combine. Stir in the chocolate.

2 Working one at a time, lay a long rectangular sheet of filo out in front of you and brush it with melted butter or oil.

3 Place a couple of teaspoons of the banana and chocolate mixture in one corner of the pastry, then fold over into a triangle shape to enclose the filling. Continue to fold in a triangular shape, until the filo is completely wrapped around the filling.

4 Make the remaining empanadas in the same way. Brush with a little more butter or oil, and dust with icing sugar and cinnamon.

5 Place on a baking sheet and bake in a preheated oven, 190°C/375°F/Gas Mark 5, for about 15 minutes or until golden. Remove from the oven and serve hot – warn people that the filling is very hot.

SERVES 4

2 sweet ripe bananas
1–2 tsp sugar
juice of ½ lemon
175–200 g/6–7 oz dark chocolate,
    broken into small pieces
about 8 sheets of filo pastry,
    halved lengthways
melted butter or vegetable oil, for brushing
icing sugar, to dust
ground cinnamon, to dust

 COOK'S TIP

You could use ready-made puff pastry instead of filo. Roll it out thinly and cut into squares. Fill, fold into triangles and seal. Bake at 200°C/400°F/Gas Mark 6 until golden.

✪✪✪ moderate
🕐 10 mins
🕐 15 mins

Melt-in-the-mouth, spicy poached pears are enveloped in a wonderfully indulgent chocolate fudge sauce and served warm.

Chocolate Fudge Pears

S E R V E S 4

4 eating pears
1–2 tbsp lemon juice
300 ml/10 fl oz water
5 tbsp caster sugar
5-cm/2-inch piece of cinnamon stick
2 cloves
200 ml/7 fl oz double cream
125 ml/4 fl oz milk
140 g/5 oz light brown sugar
2 tbsp unsalted butter, diced
2 tbsp maple syrup
200 g/7 oz dark chocolate, broken
　into pieces

1 Peel the pears using a swivel vegetable peeler. Carefully cut out the cores from the base, but leave the stalks intact because they look attractive. Brush the pears with the lemon juice to prevent discoloration.

2 Pour the water into a large, heavy-based saucepan and add the caster sugar. Stir over a low heat until the sugar has dissolved. Add the pears, cinnamon and cloves and bring to the boil. (Add a little more water if the pears are not almost covered.) Lower the heat and simmer very gently for 20 minutes.

3 Meanwhile, pour the cream and milk into another heavy-based saucepan and add the brown sugar, butter and maple syrup. Stir over a low heat until the sugar has dissolved and the butter has melted. Still stirring, bring to the boil and continue to boil, stirring constantly, for 5 minutes, until thick and smooth. Remove the pan from the heat and stir in the chocolate, a little at a time, waiting until each batch has melted before adding the next. Set aside.

4 Transfer the pears to warm individual serving plates using a slotted spoon and keep warm. Bring the poaching syrup back to the boil and cook until reduced and thickened. Remove and discard the cinnamon and cloves, then stir the syrup into the chocolate sauce. Pour the sauce over the pears and serve immediately.

⭐⭐⭐　　moderate

　　　　　10 mins

　　　　　30–35 mins

Light as air, these delicious little soufflés are the perfect choice for a dinner party dessert.

Individual Soufflés

1 Butter 6 ramekins and sprinkle with caster sugar to coat the bases and sides. Tip out any excess. Stand the ramekins on a baking tray.

2 Chop the butter and place it in a heavy-based saucepan with the chocolate. Stir over a very low heat until melted and smooth. Remove the pan from the heat and cool slightly. Beat in the egg yolks, one at a time, and stir in the orange liqueur. Set aside, stirring occasionally.

3 Gently whisk the egg whites until they are frothy, then sprinkle in the cream of tartar and whisk again rapidly until the mixture forms soft peaks. Add 1 tablespoon of caster sugar and whisk rapidly again. Add the remaining caster sugar, 1 tablespoon at a time, continuing to whisk until the whites form stiff, glossy peaks. Gently stir about one quarter of the whisked egg whites into the cooled chocolate mixture, then fold the chocolate mixture into the remaining whites using a metal spoon.

4 Divide the mixture among the ramekins and bake in a preheated oven, 220°C/425°F/Gas Mark 7, for about 10 minutes, until risen and just set. Dust with icing sugar and serve immediately, handing the sauce separately.

SERVES 4

3 tbsp caster sugar, plus 1 tbsp extra for sprinkling
140 g/5 oz unsalted butter
175 g/6 oz dark chocolate, broken into small pieces
4 large eggs, separated
2 tbsp orange liqueur
¼ tsp cream of tartar
1 tbsp icing sugar, to dust
300 ml/10 fl oz French Chocolate Sauce (see page 74), to serve

🎩 **COOK'S TIP**

If you are serving these soufflés at a dinner party, you can prepare up to Step 2 in advance, including the first step of the sauce recipe. The preparation can then be completed and the soufflé baked after the main course.

✪✪✪✪ challenging
15 mins
10 mins

Serve these sweet, soufflé-
filled, golden chocolate
crêpes with flambéed
summer berries for a
superb contrast.

Chocolate Crêpes

SERVES 6

85 g/3 oz plain flour
1 tbsp cocoa powder
1 tsp caster sugar
2 eggs, beaten lightly
175 ml/6 fl oz milk
2 tsp dark rum
2 tbsp melted unsalted butter, plus extra
   for brushing
icing sugar, to dust

filling
5 tbsp double cream
225 g/8 oz dark chocolate
3 eggs, separated
2 tbsp caster sugar

berry sauce
2 tbsp butter
4 tbsp caster sugar
150 ml/5 fl oz orange juice
225 g/8 oz berries, such as raspberries,
   blackberries and strawberries
3 tbsp white rum

⭐⭐⭐⭐ challenging
🕐 1 hr 10 mins
🕐 1 hr

1 Sift the flour, cocoa and caster sugar into a bowl. Make a well in the centre, add the eggs and beat them in a little at a time. Add the milk, rum and melted butter and beat until smooth. Cover and set aside for 30 minutes.

2 Brush an 18-cm/7-inch crêpe pan with melted butter and set over a medium heat. Pour 3 tablespoonfuls of the batter into the pan, swirling it to cover the base. Cook for 3 minutes, turning once, then slide on to a plate. Cook another 11 crêpes in the same way. Stack, interleaved with baking paper.

3 For the filling, put the cream and chocolate in a pan and melt gently, stirring. In a bowl, beat the egg yolks with half the sugar until creamy, beat in the chocolate cream and leave to cool. In a separate bowl, whisk the egg whites into soft peaks, add the rest of the sugar and beat until stiff. Stir a spoonful of the whites into the chocolate mixture, then fold in the remaining whites.

4 Spread each crêpe with 1 tablespoon of the filling, then fold in quarter. Brush with melted butter, place on a buttered baking tray and bake in a preheated oven, 200°C/400°F/Gas Mark 6, for 20 minutes.

5 For the berry sauce, melt the butter in a heavy-based frying pan over a low heat, stir in the sugar and cook until golden. Add the orange juice and cook until syrupy. Add the berries and warm through. Add the rum, heat gently for 1 minute, then ignite with a long match. Shake the pan until the flames have died down. Transfer the crêpes to plates with the sauce and serve immediately.

A warming way to end supper on a wintry evening, this steamed pudding is very easy to make.

Chocolate Pudding *with* Rum Sauce

1 Grease and flour a 1.25-litre/2-pint pudding basin. Put the butter, chocolate, sugar and vanilla in the top of a double boiler or in a heatproof bowl set over a pan of barely simmering water. Heat gently until the butter and sugar have melted, then remove from the heat and cool slightly. Beat in the eggs. Sift in the flour, stir in the milk, and mix well. Pour the mixture into the prepared pudding basin, cover the top with baking paper and pleated foil and tie with string. Steam the pudding for 1 hour, topping up with boiling water if necessary.

2 Meanwhile, make the sauce. Blend the cornflour with a little of the milk, then place in a small pan with the rest of the milk and the sugar. Stir over a medium heat until the sugar has dissolved. Bring to the boil, stirring constantly, then lower the heat and simmer until thickened and smooth. Remove from the heat and stir in the rum.

3 To serve, remove the pudding from the heat and discard the paper and foil. Run a round-bladed knife around the side of the basin, place a serving plate on top of the pudding and, holding them together, invert. Serve immediately, handing the sauce separately.

SERVES 4

4 tbsp unsalted butter
55 g/2 oz dark chocolate
115 g/4 oz caster sugar
¼ tsp vanilla essence
2 eggs, beaten lightly
175 g/6 oz self-raising flour
5 tbsp milk

rum sauce
2 tbsp cornflour
300 ml/10 fl oz milk
2 tbsp caster sugar
2 tbsp dark rum

🍳 COOK'S TIP

You could add 2 tablespoons of rum to the pudding in place of some of the milk, if you like.

⭐⭐ easy
🕐 15 mins
🕐 1 hr

The sharpness of the apple and cranberries contrasts deliciously with the sweetness of the chocolate in this wonderful, fluffy sponge pudding.

Chocolate Cranberry Sponge

SERVES 4

4 tbsp dark brown sugar, plus 2 tsp extra
    for sprinkling
1 large cooking apple
85 g/3 oz cranberries, thawed if frozen
4 tbsp unsalted butter
2 eggs, beaten lightly
85 g/3 oz self-raising flour
3 tbsp cocoa powder

sauce
175 g/6 oz dark chocolate, broken into pieces
400 ml/14 fl oz evaporated milk
1 tsp vanilla essence
½ tsp almond essence

1 Grease a 1.25-litre/2-pint pudding basin, sprinkle with brown sugar to coat the sides and tip out any excess. Peel, core and dice the apple and mix with the cranberries. Put the fruit in the prepared pudding basin.

2 Place the butter, brown sugar and eggs in a large bowl. Sift in the flour and cocoa and beat well until thoroughly mixed. Pour the mixture into the basin on top of the fruit, cover the top with paper and foil and tie with string. Steam the pudding for about 1 hour, until risen, topping up with additional boiling water if necessary.

3 Meanwhile, make the sauce. Put the dark chocolate and evaporated milk in the top of a double boiler or a heatproof bowl set over a pan of barely simmering water. Stir until the chocolate has melted, then remove from the heat. Whisk in the vanilla and almond essences and continue to beat until the sauce is thick and smooth.

4 To serve, remove the pudding from the heat. Run a round-bladed knife around the side of the basin, place a serving plate on top of the pudding and, holding them securely together, invert. Serve immediately, handing the sauce separately.

COOK'S TIP

When cranberries are unavailable, you could use blackcurrants, blueberries or raspberries in their place.

easy

25 mins

1 hr

This creamy white chocolate sauce adds a touch of luxury and sophistication to the dinner table. Serve with ice cream or chocolate sponge.

White Chocolate Fudge Sauce

1 Pour the cream into the top of a double boiler or a heatproof bowl set over a pan of barely simmering water. Add the butter and sugar and stir until the mixture is smooth. Remove from the heat.

2 Stir in the chocolate, a few pieces at a time, waiting until each batch has melted before adding the next. Add the brandy and stir the sauce until smooth. Cool to room temperature before serving.

MAKES 225 ML/8 FL OZ

150 ml/5 fl oz double cream
4 tbsp unsalted butter, diced
3 tbsp caster sugar
175 g/6 oz white chocolate, broken into pieces
2 tbsp brandy

COOK'S TIP

Dark or milk chocolate can also be used in this recipe.

very easy

5 mins, plus 20 mins

10–15 mins

CHOCOLATE

This rich, warm – and alcoholic – sauce is superb with both hot and cold desserts and positively magical with ice cream.

French Chocolate Sauce

MAKES 150 ML/5 FL OZ

6 tbsp double cream
85 g/3 oz dark chocolate, broken into small pieces
2 tbsp orange liqueur

1 Bring the cream gently to the boil in a small, heavy-based saucepan over a low heat. Remove the pan from the heat, add the chocolate and stir until melted and smooth.

2 Stir in the liqueur and serve immediately or keep the sauce warm in a heatproof bowl set over a pan of simmering water until required.

⊕ COOK'S TIP

Try using different flavours of liqueur, such as mint or coffee.

⭐ very easy

🕐 5 mins

🕐 10–15 mins

This simple sauce is a deliciously rich accompaniment to hot and cold desserts and is suitable for all the family.

Glossy Chocolate Sauce

1 Put the sugar and water in a small, heavy-based pan set over a low heat and stir until the sugar has dissolved. Stir in the chocolate, a few pieces at a time, waiting until each batch has melted before adding the next. Stir in the butter, a few pieces at a time, waiting until each batch has been incorporated before adding the next. Do not allow the sauce to boil.

2 Stir in the orange juice and remove the pan from the heat. Serve immediately or keep warm until required.

MAKES 150 ML/5 FL OZ

100 g/3½ oz caster sugar
4 tbsp water
175 g/6 oz dark chocolate, broken into pieces
2 tbsp unsalted butter, diced
2 tbsp orange juice

COOK'S TIP

To freeze the sauce, leave it to cool, transfer to a freezer-proof container and freeze for up to three months. Defrost at room temperature before reheating.

very easy

5 mins

10–15 mins

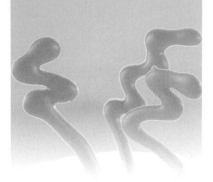

Cold Desserts

Cool, creamy, sumptuous and indulgent are just a few of the words that spring to mind when you think of cold chocolate desserts. The desserts contained in this chapter are a combination of all of these.

Some of the desserts are surprisingly quick and simple to make, while others are more elaborate. One of the best things about these desserts is they can all be made in advance, sometimes days in advance, making them perfect for entertaining. A quick decoration when necessary is all that is needed on the day. Even the Baked Chocolate Alaska can be assembled in advance and popped into the oven just before serving.

The classic combination of chocolate and mint flavours makes an attractive dessert for special occasions.

Chocolate Mint Swirl

SERVES 6

300 ml/10 fl oz double cream
150 ml/5 fl oz creamy fromage frais
2 tbsp icing sugar
1 tbsp crème de menthe
175 g/6 oz dark chocolate, to decorate

1 Place the cream in a large mixing bowl and whisk until standing in soft peaks.

2 Fold in the fromage frais and icing sugar, then place about one third of the mixture in a smaller bowl. Stir the crème de menthe into the smaller bowl. Stir the melted chocolate into the larger bowl.

3 Place alternate spoonfuls of the 2 mixtures in serving glasses, then swirl the mixture together. Chill until required.

4 To make the piped chocolate decorations, melt a small amount of chocolate and place in a paper piping bag.

5 Place a sheet of baking paper on a board and pipe squiggles, stars or flower shapes with the melted chocolate. Alternatively, to make curved decorations, pipe decorations on to a long strip of baking paper, then carefully place the strip over a rolling pin, securing with sticky tape. Leave the chocolate to set, then carefully remove from the baking paper.

6 Decorate each dessert with piped chocolate decorations and serve.

easy
45 mins
5 mins

🍳 COOK'S TIP

Pipe the patterns freehand, as described above, or draw patterns on to baking paper first, turn the parchment over and then pipe the chocolate, following the drawn outline.

Wickedly rich, these little chocolate pots, flavoured with just a hint of dark rum, are pure indulgence on any occasion!

Chocolate Rum Pots

1 Melt the chocolate and leave to cool slightly.

2 Whisk the egg yolks with the caster sugar in a bowl until pale and fluffy, using an electric whisk or balloon whisk.

3 Drizzle the chocolate into the mixture and fold in together with the rum and the double cream.

4 Whisk the egg whites in a separate bowl until standing in soft peaks. Fold the egg whites into the chocolate mixture in 2 batches. Divide the mixture between 6 ramekins or other individual dishes and chill for at least 2 hours.

5 To serve, decorate with marbled chocolate shapes.

SERVES 6

225 g/8 oz dark chocolate
4 eggs, separated
6 tbsp caster sugar
4 tbsp dark rum
4 tbsp double cream
marbled chocolate shapes (see page 108), to decorate

 COOK'S TIP

Make sure you use a perfectly grease-free bowl and whisk for whisking the egg whites. They will not aerate if any grease is present as the smallest amount breaks down the bubbles in the whites, preventing them from holding air.

⭐⭐ easy
2 hrs 20 mins
5 mins

These creamy chocolate- and coffee-flavoured desserts make a perfect end to a fine meal.

Mocha Creams

SERVES 4

225 g/8 oz dark chocolate
1 tbsp instant coffee
300 ml/10 fl oz boiling water
1 sachet gelatine
3 tbsp cold water
1 tsp vanilla essence
1 tbsp coffee-flavoured liqueur (optional)
300 ml/10 fl oz double cream
4 chocolate coffee beans, to decorate
8 amaretti biscuits, to serve

1 Break the chocolate into small pieces and place in a saucepan with the coffee. Add the boiling water and heat gently, stirring constantly, until the chocolate has melted.

2 Sprinkle the gelatine over the cold water and leave to go spongy, then whisk it into the hot chocolate mixture to dissolve it.

3 Stir in the vanilla and coffee-flavoured liqueur, if using. Leave to stand in a cool place until just beginning to thicken, whisking from time to time.

4 Whisk the cream until it is standing in soft peaks. Reserve a little for decorating the desserts and fold the remainder into the chocolate mixture. Spoon into serving dishes and leave to set.

5 Decorate with the reserved cream and coffee beans and serve with the amaretti biscuits.

🍴 COOK'S TIP

To add a delicious almond flavour to the dessert, replace the coffee-flavoured liqueur with almond-flavoured (amaretto) liqueur.

⭐⭐ easy

🕐 30 mins

🕐 5 mins

Three layers of rich mousse give this elegant dessert extra chocolate appeal. It is a little fiddly to prepare, but well worth the extra effort.

Layered Chocolate Mousse

1 Line a 450-g/1-lb loaf tin with baking paper. Separate the eggs, putting each egg white in a separate bowl. Place the egg yolks, cornflour and sugar in a large mixing bowl and whisk until well combined. Place the milk in a pan and heat gently, stirring until almost boiling. Pour the milk on to the egg yolks, whisking.

2 Set the bowl over a pan of gently simmering water and cook, stirring, until the mixture thickens enough to thinly coat the back of a wooden spoon.

3 Sprinkle the gelatine over the water in a small heatproof bowl and leave to go spongy. Place over a pan of hot water and stir until dissolved. Stir into the hot egg yolk mixture. Leave to cool.

4 Whip the cream until just holding its shape. Fold it into the egg custard, then divide the mixture into 3. Melt the 3 types of chocolate separately. Fold the dark chocolate into one egg custard portion. Whisk one egg white until standing in soft peaks and fold into the dark chocolate custard until thoroughly combined. Pour into the prepared tin and level the top. Chill in the coldest part of the refrigerator until just set. Leave the remaining mixtures at room temperature.

5 Fold the white chocolate into another portion of the egg custard. Whisk another egg white and fold in. Pour on top of the dark chocolate layer and chill quickly. Repeat with the remaining milk chocolate and egg white. Chill for at least 2 hours until set. To serve, carefully turn out on to a serving dish and decorate with chocolate Caraque.

SERVES 8

3 eggs
1 tsp cornflour
4 tbsp caster sugar
300 ml/10 fl oz milk
1 sachet gelatine
3 tbsp water
300 ml/10 fl oz double cream
75 g/2¾ oz dark chocolate
75 g/2¾ oz white chocolate
75 g/2¾ oz milk chocolate
chocolate Caraque, to decorate
   (see page 15)

✪✪✪   moderate

3 hrs

10 mins

This classic French dish
is part way between a
mousse and a parfait. It is
usually chilled in a large
mould, but here it is made
in individual moulds.

Chocolate Marquise

SERVES 6

200 g/7 oz dark chocolate
100 g/3½ oz butter
3 egg yolks
75 g/2¾ oz caster sugar
1 tsp chocolate essence or 1 tbsp chocolate-
    flavoured liqueur
300 ml/10 fl oz double cream

to serve
chocolate-dipped fruits
crème fraîche
cocoa powder, to dust

1 Break the chocolate into pieces. Place the chocolate and butter in a bowl over a pan of gently simmering water and stir until melted and well combined. Remove from the heat and leave to cool.

2 Place the egg yolks in a mixing bowl with the sugar and whisk until pale and fluffy. Using an electric whisk on low speed, whisk in the cool chocolate mixture. Stir in the chocolate essence or chocolate-flavoured liqueur.

3 Whip the cream until just holding its shape. Fold into the chocolate mixture. Spoon into 6 small ramekins, or individual metal moulds. Leave to chill for at least 2 hours.

4 To serve, turn out the desserts on to individual serving dishes. If you have difficulty turning them out, dip the moulds into a bowl of warm water for a few seconds to help the marquise to slip out. Serve with chocolate-dipped fruit and crème fraîche and dust with cocoa powder.

 COOK'S TIP

The slight tartness of the crème fraîche contrasts well with this very rich dessert. Dip the fruit in white chocolate to give a good colour contrast.

easy
2hrs 30 mins
5 mins

This iced dessert is somewhere between a chocolate mousse and an ice cream. Serve it with a chocolate sauce or a fruit coulis and fresh fruit.

Iced White Chocolate Terrine

1 Line a 450-g/1-lb loaf tin with foil or clingfilm, pressing out as many creases as you can.

2 Place the granulated sugar and water in a heavy-based pan and heat gently, stirring until the sugar has dissolved. Bring to the boil and boil for 1–2 minutes until syrupy, then remove the pan from the heat.

3 Break the white chocolate into small pieces and stir it into the syrup, continuing to stir until the chocolate has melted and combined with the syrup. Leave to cool slightly.

4 Beat the egg yolks into the chocolate mixture. Leave to cool completely.

5 Lightly whip the cream until just holding its shape and fold it into the chocolate mixture.

6 Whisk the egg whites in a separate bowl until they are standing in soft peaks. Fold into the chocolate mixture. Pour into the prepared loaf tin and freeze overnight.

7 To serve, remove from the freezer about 10–15 minutes before serving. Turn out of the tin and cut into slices before serving.

SERVES **8**

2 tbsp granulated sugar
5 tbsp water
300 g/10½ oz white chocolate
3 eggs, separated
300 ml/10 fl oz double cream

to serve
chocolate sauce or fruit coulis
fresh berries

🖰 COOK'S TIP

To make a coulis, place 225 g/8 oz soft fruit of your choice in a food processor. Add 1–2 tablespoons icing sugar and blend to a purée. If the fruit contains seeds, push the purée through a sieve to remove them.

★★★   moderate

◔   12 hrs 50 mins

🕐   55 mins

A banana split in a glass! Choose the best vanilla ice cream you can find, or better still, make your own.

Chocolate Banana Sundae

SERVES 4

glossy chocolate sauce
55 g/2 oz dark chocolate
4 tbsp golden syrup
1 tbsp butter
1 tbsp brandy or rum (optional)

sundae
4 bananas
150 ml/5 fl oz double cream
8–12 scoops of good quality vanilla ice cream
75 g/2¾ oz flaked or chopped almonds, toasted
grated or flaked chocolate, to sprinkle
4 fan wafer biscuits, to serve

1 To make the chocolate sauce, break the chocolate into small pieces and place in a heatproof bowl with the syrup and butter. Heat over a pan of hot water until melted, stirring until well combined. Remove the bowl from the heat and stir in the brandy or rum, if using.

2 Slice the bananas and whip the cream until just holding its shape. Place a scoop of ice cream in the bottom of each of 4 tall sundae dishes. Top with slices of banana, some chocolate sauce, a spoonful of cream and a good sprinkling of nuts.

3 Repeat the layers, finishing with a good dollop of cream. Sprinkle with nuts and a little grated or flaked chocolate. Serve with fan wafer biscuits.

⭐⭐ easy
🕐 15 mins
🕐 5 mins

👨‍🍳 COOK'S TIP

For a traditional banana split, halve the bananas lengthways and place on a plate with two scoops of ice cream between. Top with cream and sprinkle with nuts. Serve with the glossy chocolate sauce poured over the top.

A cool dessert that leaves the cook completely unflustered – assemble it in advance and freeze until required.

Baked Chocolate Alaska

1 Grease an 18-cm/7-inch round cake tin and line the base with baking paper.

2 Whisk the eggs and caster sugar in a bowl until very thick and pale. Sift the flour and cocoa powder together and carefully fold in.

3 Pour into the prepared tin and bake in a preheated oven, 220°C/425°F/Gas Mark 7, for 7 minutes or until springy to the touch. Transfer to a wire rack to cool completely. Leave the oven on

4 Whisk the egg whites in a clean bowl until they are standing in soft peaks. Gradually add the sugar, whisking until you have a thick, glossy meringue.

5 Place the sponge on a baking tray and pile the ice cream on to the centre in a heaped dome.

6 Pipe or spread the meringue over the ice cream, making sure the ice cream is completely enclosed. (At this point the dessert can be frozen, if wished.)

7 Return it to the oven for about 5 minutes, until the meringue is just golden. Serve immediately.

SERVES 4

2 eggs
4 tbsp caster sugar
5 tbsp plain flour
2 tbsp cocoa powder
1 litre/1¾ pints good quality chocolate
    ice cream

meringue
3 egg whites
150 g/5½ oz caster sugar

 COOK'S TIP

This dessert is delicious served with a blackcurrant coulis. Cook a few blackcurrants in a little orange juice until soft, purée and push through a sieve, then sweeten to taste with a little icing sugar.

★★★ moderate
🕑 50 mins
🕒 12 mins

A rich chocolate ice cream, delicious on its own or served with chocolate sauce. For a special dessert, serve it in these attractive trellis shells.

Rich Chocolate Ice Cream

SERVES **6**

1 egg
3 egg yolks
85 g/3 oz caster sugar
300 ml/10 fl oz milk
250 g/9 oz dark chocolate
300 ml/10 fl oz double cream

trellis shells
200 g/7 oz dark chocolate

1 Beat together the egg, egg yolks and caster sugar in a mixing bowl until well combined. Heat the milk until it is almost boiling.

2 Gradually pour the hot milk on to the eggs, whisking as you do so. Place the bowl over a pan of gently simmering water and cook, stirring, until the mixture thickens sufficiently to thinly coat the back of a wooden spoon.

3 Break the dark chocolate into small pieces and add to the hot custard. Stir until the chocolate has melted. Cover with a sheet of dampened baking paper and leave until cold.

4 Whip the cream until just holding its shape, then fold into the cold chocolate custard. Transfer to a freezer-proof container and freeze for 1–2 hours, until the mixture is frozen 2.5 cm/1 inch from the sides.

5 Scrape the ice cream into a chilled bowl and beat again until smooth. Re-freeze until firm.

6 Meanwhile, make the trellis shells: invert 2 muffin trays and cover 12 alternate mounds with clingfilm. Melt the chocolate, place it in a paper piping bag and snip off the end.

7 Pipe a circle around the base of the mound, then pipe chocolate back and forth over it to form a trellis; carefully pipe a double thickness. Pipe around the base again. Chill until set, then lift from the tray and remove the clingfilm. Serve the ice cream in the trellis shells.

moderate

4–5 hrs

12 mins

This white chocolate ice cream is served in a biscuit cup. If desired, top with a chocolate sauce for a true chocolate addict's treat.

White Chocolate Ice Cream

1 Place baking paper on 2 baking trays. To make the ice cream, beat the egg, egg yolk and sugar. Break the chocolate into pieces, place in a bowl with 3 tablespoons of the milk and melt over a pan of hot water. Heat the remaining milk until almost boiling and pour on to the eggs, whisking. Place over a pan of simmering water and cook, stirring, until the mixture thickens enough to coat the back of a wooden spoon. Whisk in the chocolate. Cover with dampened baking paper and leave until cold.

2 Whip the cream until just holding its shape and fold into the custard. Transfer to a freezer-proof container and freeze the mixture for 1–2 hours, until frozen 2.5 cm/1 inch from the sides. Scrape into a bowl and beat again until smooth. Re-freeze until firm.

3 To make the cups, beat the egg white and sugar together. Beat in the flour and cocoa, then the butter. Place 1 tablespoon of mixture on one tray; spread out to a 13-cm/5-inch circle. Bake in a preheated oven, 200°C/400°F/Gas Mark 6, for 4–5 minutes. Remove and mould over an upturned cup. Leave to set, then cool on a wire rack. Repeat to make 6 cups. Serve the ice cream in the biscuit cups.

SERVES 6

1 egg
1 egg yolk
3 tbsp caster sugar
150 g/5½ oz white chocolate
300 ml/10 fl oz milk
150 ml/5 fl oz double cream

biscuit cups
1 egg white
4 tbsp caster sugar
2 tbsp plain flour, sifted
2 tbsp cocoa powder, sifted
2 tbsp butter, melted

🍴 COOK'S TIP

Transfer the ice cream to the refrigerator about 20 minutes before it is required, so that it can soften slightly. However, do not scoop it into the biscuit cups until ready to serve.

★★★   moderate
🕐   4–5 hrs
🕐   15 mins

This chocolate dessert, consisting of a rich chocolate mousse-like filling enclosed in boudoir biscuits, is a variation of a popular classic.

Chocolate Charlotte

SERVES 8

about 22 boudoir biscuits
4 tbsp orange-flavoured liqueur
250 g/9 oz dark chocolate, melted
150 ml/5 fl oz double cream
4 eggs
150 g/5½ oz caster sugar

to decorate
150 ml/5 fl oz whipping cream
2 tbsp caster sugar
½ tsp vanilla essence
dark chocolate Quick Curls (see page 15)

1 Line the base of a Charlotte mould or a deep 18-cm/7-inch round cake tin with a piece of baking paper.

2 Place the boudoir biscuits on a tray and sprinkle with half of the orange-flavoured liqueur. Use to line the sides of the mould or tin, trimming if necessary to make a tight fit.

3 Mix the melted chocolate with the double cream. Separate the eggs and place the whites in a large grease-free bowl. Beat the egg yolks into the chocolate mixture.

4 Whisk the egg whites until standing in stiff peaks, then gradually add the caster sugar, whisking until stiff and glossy. Carefully fold the egg whites into the chocolate mixture in 2 batches, taking care not to knock out the air. Pour into the centre of the mould. Trim the biscuits so that they are level with the chocolate mixture. Chill for at least 5 hours.

5 To decorate, whisk the cream, sugar and vanilla essence until standing in soft peaks. Turn out the charlotte on to a serving dish. Pipe cream rosettes around the base and decorate with chocolate Quick Curls and other decorations of your choice.

⭐⭐⭐ moderate

🕐 5 hrs 40 mins

🕐 5 mins

Dark and white chocolate cheesecake fillings are marbled together to give an attractive finish to this rich and decadent dessert.

Marbled Cheesecake

1 Place the toasted oat cereal in a plastic bag and crush with a rolling pin. Pour the crushed cereal into a mixing bowl and stir in the hazelnuts.

2 Melt the butter and chocolate together over a low heat and add to the cereal mixture, stirring until well coated.

3 Using the bottom of a glass, press the mixture into the base and up the sides of a 20 cm/8-inch springform tin.

4 Beat together the cheese and sugar with a wooden spoon until smooth. Beat in the yogurt. Whip the cream until just holding its shape and fold into the mixture. Sprinkle the gelatine over the water in a heatproof bowl and leave to go spongy. Place over a pan of hot water and stir until dissolved. Stir into the mixture.

5 Divide the mixture in half and beat the dark chocolate into one half and the white chocolate into the other half.

6 Place alternate spoonfuls of mixture on top of the cereal base. Swirl the filling together with the tip of a knife to give a marbled effect. Level the top with a scraper or a spatula. Chill for at least 2 hours to set before serving.

SERVES 10

base
225 g/8 oz toasted oat cereal
50 g/1¾ oz toasted hazelnuts, chopped
4 tbsp butter
25 g/1 oz dark chocolate

filling
350 g/12 oz full-fat soft cheese
100 g/3½ oz caster sugar
200 ml/7 fl oz thick yogurt
300 ml/10 fl oz double cream
1 sachet gelatine
3 tbsp water
175 g/6 oz dark chocolate, melted
175 g/6 oz white chocolate, melted

🍳 **COOK'S TIP**

If you prefer to use leaf gelatine, you will need about 2½ leaves. Follow the instructions on the packet for dissolving them.

 ✪✪✪ moderate
🕐 2 hrs 30 mins
🕐 5 mins

The exotic combination of banana and coconut goes well with chocolate. Fresh coconut gives a better flavour than desiccated coconut.

Banana Coconut Cheesecake

SERVES 10

225 g/8 oz chocolate chip cookies
4 tbsp melted butter
350 g/12 oz medium-fat soft cheese
75 g/2¾ oz caster sugar
50 g/1¾ oz fresh coconut, grated
2 tbsp coconut-flavoured liqueur
2 ripe bananas
125 g/4½ oz dark chocolate
1 sachet gelatine
3 tbsp water
150 ml/5 fl oz double cream

to decorate
1 banana
lemon juice
a little melted chocolate

1 Place the cookies in a plastic bag and crush with a rolling pin. Tip into a mixing bowl and stir in the melted butter. Firmly press the biscuit mixture into the base and up the sides of a 20-cm/8-inch springform tin.

2 Beat together the soft cheese and caster sugar until well combined, then beat in the grated fresh coconut and coconut-flavoured liqueur. Mash the bananas and beat them in. Melt the dark chocolate in a heatproof bowl set over a pan of barely simmering water and then beat in to the soft cheese mixture until well combined.

3 Sprinkle the gelatine over the water in a heatproof bowl and leave to go spongy. Place over a pan of hot water and stir until dissolved. Stir into the chocolate mixture. Whisk the cream until just holding its shape and stir into the chocolate mixture. Spoon over the base and chill for 2 hours, until set.

4 To serve, carefully transfer to a serving plate. Slice the banana, toss in lemon juice and arrange around the edge of the cheesecake. Drizzle with melted chocolate and leave to set.

moderate
2 hrs 30 mins
5 mins

COOK'S TIP

To crack the coconut, pierce 2 of the 'eyes' and drain off the liquid. Tap hard around the centre with a hammer until it cracks, then lever apart.

A crumbly ginger chocolate base topped with velvety smooth chocolate brandy cream makes this a blissful cake.

Chocolate Brandy Torte

1 Crush the biscuits in a bag with a rolling pin or in a food processor. Melt the chocolate and butter together and pour over the biscuits. Mix well, then use to line the base and sides of a 23-cm/9-inch loose-bottomed flan tin or springform tin. Leave to chill while preparing the filling.

2 To make the filling, melt the dark chocolate in a heatproof bowl set over a pan of barely simmering water, remove from the heat and beat in the mascarpone cheese, egg yolks and brandy.

3 Lightly whip the cream until just holding its shape and gently fold in the chocolate mixture.

4 Whisk the egg whites in a grease-free bowl until standing in soft peaks. Add the caster sugar a little at a time and whisk until thick and glossy. Fold into the chocolate mixture, in 2 batches, until just mixed.

5 Spoon the mixture into the prepared base and chill for at least 2 hours. Carefully transfer to a serving plate. To decorate, whip the cream and pipe swirls on to the torte. Top with the chocolate coffee beans. Sprinkle with a little grated chocolate.

SERVES 12

base
250 g/9 oz gingernut biscuits
75 g/2¾ oz dark chocolate
100 g/3½ oz butter

filling
225 g/8 oz dark chocolate, broken into pieces
250 g/9 oz mascarpone cheese
2 eggs, separated
3 tbsp brandy
300 ml/10 fl oz double cream
4 tbsp caster sugar

to decorate
100 ml/3½ fl oz double cream
chocolate coffee beans
grated chocolate

🎩 **COOK'S TIP**

If chocolate coffee beans are unavailable, use chocolate-coated raisins or pieces of stem ginger to decorate.

⭐⭐   easy
🕐   2 hrs 40 mins
🕐   5 mins

CHOCOLATE

Stacks of crisp shortcake are sandwiched with chocolate-flavoured cream and fresh raspberries, and served with a fresh raspberry coulis.

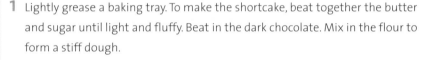

Chocolate Shortcake Towers

SERVES 6

shortcake
225 g/8 oz butter
75 g/2¾ oz light muscovado sugar
50 g/1¾ oz dark chocolate, grated
275 g/9½ oz plain flour, sifted, plus extra for dusting

to finish
350 g/12 oz fresh raspberries
2 tbsp icing sugar
300 ml/10 fl oz double cream
3 tbsp milk
100 g/3½ oz white chocolate, melted
icing sugar, to dust

1 Lightly grease a baking tray. To make the shortcake, beat together the butter and sugar until light and fluffy. Beat in the dark chocolate. Mix in the flour to form a stiff dough.

2 Roll out the dough on a lightly floured surface and stamp out 18 rounds with a 7.5-cm/3-inch biscuit cutter. Place the rounds on the baking tray and bake in a preheated oven, 200°C/400°F/Gas Mark 6, for 10 minutes, until crisp and golden. Leave to cool on the tray.

3 To make the coulis, set aside about 100 g/3½ oz of the raspberries. Purée the remainder in a food processor with the icing sugar, then push through a sieve to remove the seeds. Chill. Set aside 2 teaspoons of the cream. Whip the remainder until just holding its shape. Fold in the milk and the melted chocolate.

4 For each tower, spoon a little coulis on to a serving plate. Drop small dots of the reserved cream into the coulis around the edge of the plate and use a skewer to drag through the cream to make an attractive pattern.

5 Place a shortcake circle on the plate and spoon on a little of the chocolate cream. Top with 2 or 3 raspberries, top with another shortcake and repeat. Place a third biscuit on top. Dust with icing sugar and serve immediately.

⭐⭐⭐   moderate

🕐   30 mins

🕐   10 mins

Combine all the delightful flavours of a Black Forest gâteau in this new guise – the results are stunning.

Black Forest Trifle

1 Place the slices of chocolate Swiss roll in the bottom of a glass serving bowl.

2 Drain the black cherries, reserving 6 tablespoons of the juice. Place the cherries and the reserved juice on top of the cake. Sprinkle with the kirsch.

3 In a bowl, mix the cornflour and caster sugar. Stir in enough of the milk to mix to a smooth paste. Beat in the egg yolks and the whole egg.

4 Heat the remaining milk in a small saucepan until almost boiling, then gradually pour it on to the egg mixture, whisking well until it is combined.

5 Place the bowl over a pan of hot water and cook over a low heat until the custard thickens, stirring. Add the chocolate and stir until melted.

6 Pour the chocolate custard over the cherries and cool. When cold, spread the cream over the custard, swirling with the back of a spoon. Chill thoroughly before decorating.

7 Decorate with chocolate caraque and whole maraschino cherries, if using, before serving.

COOK'S TIP

The Black Forest gâteau, or Schwarzwälder Kirschtorte, originates from southern Germany, and would have been made with about a cupful of kirsch (cherry liqueur).

SERVES 6

6 thin slices chocolate butter cream Swiss roll
800 g/1 lb 12 oz canned black cherries in juice
2 tbsp kirsch
1 tbsp cornflour
2 tbsp caster sugar
425 ml/15 fl oz milk
3 egg yolks
1 egg
75 g/2¾ oz dark chocolate
300 ml/10 fl oz double cream, whipped lightly

to decorate
dark chocolate Caraque (see page 15)
maraschino cherries (optional)

moderate
1 hr 30 mins
10 mins

Any dry sparkling wine made by the traditional method used for Champagne can be used for this elegant dessert.

Champagne Mousse

SERVES 4

sponge
4 eggs
100 g/3½ oz caster sugar
75 g/2¾ oz self-raising flour
2 tbsp cocoa powder
2 tbsp butter, melted

mousse
1 sachet gelatine
3 tbsp water
300 ml/10 fl oz Champagne
300 ml/10 fl oz double cream
2 egg whites
6 tbsp caster sugar

to decorate
55 g/2 oz dark chocolate-flavoured cake
    covering, melted

1 Line a 38 x 25-cm/15 x 10-inch Swiss roll tin with greased baking paper. Place the eggs and sugar in a bowl and beat with an electric whisk until the mixture is very thick and the whisk leaves a trail when lifted. If using a balloon whisk, stand the bowl over a pan of hot water while whisking. Sift the flour and cocoa together and fold into the egg mixture. Fold in the butter. Pour into the tin and bake in a preheated oven, 200°C/400°F/Gas Mark 6, for 8 minutes or until springy to the touch. Cool for 5 minutes, then turn out on to a wire rack and leave until completely cold.

2 Line four 10-cm/4-inch baking rings with baking paper. Line the sides of the rings with 2.5-cm/1-inch strips of cake and the base with circles.

3 To make the mousse, sprinkle the gelatine over the water in a heatproof bowl and leave to go spongy. Place the bowl over a pan of hot water and stir until dissolved. Stir in the Champagne.

4 Whip the cream until just holding its shape. Fold in the Champagne mixture. Set aside in a cool place until on the point of setting, stirring occasionally. Whisk the egg whites until standing in soft peaks, add the sugar and whisk until glossy. Fold into the setting mixture. Spoon into the sponge cases, allowing the mixture to go above the sponge. Chill for 2 hours. Pipe the melted cake covering in squiggles on a piece of baking paper, leave them to set, then use them to decorate the mousses.

challenging

3 hrs 15 mins

8 mins

Hidden in a ring of chocolate sponge lies the secret of this freezer cake – chocolate mint ice cream. Use orange or coffee ice cream if preferred.

Chocolate Freezer Cake

1 Lightly grease a 23-cm/9-inch ring tin. Place the eggs and sugar in a large mixing bowl. If using an electric whisk, whisk the mixture until it is very thick and the whisk leaves a trail. If using a balloon whisk, stand the bowl over a pan of hot water while whisking.

2 Sift the flour and cocoa together and fold into the egg mixture. Pour into the prepared tin and bake in a preheated oven, 180°C/350°F/Gas Mark 4, for 30 minutes or until springy to the touch. Leave to cool in the tin for a few minutes before turning out on to a wire rack to cool completely.

3 Wash and dry the cake tin and line with a strip of clingfilm, overhanging slightly. Invert the cake so it is base-side up, and carefully cut off the top 1 cm/½ inch in one slice. Set aside.

4 Return the cake to the tin. Using a spoon, scoop out the centre of the cake, leaving a shell approximately 1 cm/½ inch thick.

5 Remove the ice cream from the freezer and leave to stand for a few minutes, then beat with a wooden spoon until softened a little. Fill the centre of the cake with the ice cream, levelling the top. Replace the top of the cake.

6 Cover with the overhanging clingfilm and freeze for at least 2 hours.

7 To serve, turn the cake out on to a serving dish and drizzle over some of the chocolate sauce in an attractive pattern, if you wish. Cut the cake into slices and serve with the remaining sauce.

SERVES 8

4 eggs
175 g/6 oz caster sugar
100 g/3½ oz self-raising flour
3 tbsp cocoa powder
500 ml/17 fl oz chocolate and mint ice cream
Glossy Chocolate Sauce (see page 75)

easy
3 hrs
30 mins

An all-time favourite with chocoholics – the 'mud' refers to the gooey, rich chocolate layer of the cake.

Mississippi Mud Pie

SERVES 8

225 g/8 oz plain flour, plus flour for dusting
2 tbsp cocoa powder
150 g/5½ oz butter
2 tbsp caster sugar
about 2 tbsp cold water

filling
175 g/6 oz butter
350 g/12 oz dark muscovado sugar
4 eggs, beaten lightly
4 tbsp cocoa powder, sifted
150 g/5½ oz dark chocolate, melted
300ml/10 fl oz single cream
1 tsp chocolate essence

to decorate
425 ml/15 fl oz double cream, whipped
chocolate flakes and Quick Curls
    (see page 15)

1 To make the pastry, sift the flour and cocoa powder into a mixing bowl. Rub in the butter until the mixture resembles fine breadcrumbs. Stir in the sugar and enough cold water to mix to a soft dough. Chill for 15 minutes.

2 Roll out the pastry dough on a lightly floured surface and use to line a deep 23-cm/9-inch loose-bottomed flan tin or ceramic flan dish. Line with foil or baking paper and baking beans. Bake blind in a preheated oven, 190°C/375°F/Gas Mark 5, for 15 minutes. Remove the beans and foil or paper and cook for a further 10 minutes, until crisp.

3 Meanwhile, make the filling. Beat the butter and sugar in a bowl and gradually beat in the eggs with the cocoa powder. Beat in the melted chocolate with the single cream and the chocolate essence.

4 Pour the mixture into the cooked pastry case and bake at 170°C/325°F/Gas Mark 3 for 45 minutes or until the filling is set.

5 Leave to cool completely, then transfer the pie to a serving plate, if preferred. Cover with the whipped cream and leave to chill.

6 Decorate the pie with chocolate flakes and quick chocolate curls.

moderate
3 hrs 30 mins
1 hr 10 mins

🍳 **COOK'S TIP**

Ceramic or metal baking beans are available from kitchen shops. Alternatively, you can use dried beans kept specifically for the purpose.

Chocolate profiteroles are a popular choice for a special occasion dessert. In this recipe they are filled with a delicious banana-flavoured cream – the perfect combination!

Banana Cream Profiteroles

1 Lightly grease a baking tray and sprinkle with a little water. To make the pastry, place the water in a pan. Cut the butter into small pieces and add to the pan. Heat gently until the butter melts, then bring to a rolling boil. Remove the pan from the heat and add the flour in one go, beating well until the mixture leaves the sides of the pan and forms a ball. Leave to cool slightly, then gradually beat in the eggs to form a smooth, glossy mixture. Spoon the choux paste into a large piping bag fitted with a 1-cm/½-inch plain nozzle.

2 Pipe about 18 small balls of the paste on to the baking tray, allowing enough room for them to expand during cooking. Bake in a preheated oven, 220°C/425°F/Gas Mark 7, for 15–20 minutes, until crisp and golden. Remove from the oven and make a small slit in each one for the steam to escape. Cool on a wire rack.

3 To make the chocolate sauce, place all the ingredients in a heatproof bowl, set over a pan of simmering water and heat until combined and smooth, stirring constantly.

4 To make the filling, whip the cream until standing in soft peaks. Mash the banana with the sugar and liqueur. Fold into the cream. Place in a piping bag fitted with a 1-cm/½-inch plain nozzle and pipe into the profiteroles. Serve with the sauce poured over.

SERVES 4

choux pastry
150 ml/5 fl oz water
5 tbsp butter
90 g/3 oz strong plain flour, sifted
2 eggs

chocolate sauce
100 g/3½ oz dark chocolate, broken into pieces
2 tbsp water
4 tbsp icing sugar
2 tbsp unsalted butter

filling
300 ml/10 fl oz double cream
1 banana
2 tbsp icing sugar
2 tbsp banana-flavoured liqueur

✪✪✪✪ challenging
45 mins
15 20 mins

This is a modern version
of the well-known and
traditional chocolate
dessert from Italy.

Tiramisu Layers

SERVES 4

150 ml/5 fl oz double cream
400 g/14 oz mascarpone cheese
300 g/10½ oz dark chocolate, melted
400 ml/14 fl oz black coffee with 4 tbsp
    caster sugar, cooled
6 tbsp dark rum or brandy
36 sponge fingers, about 400 g/14 oz
cocoa powder, to dust

1 Whip the cream until it just holds its shape. Stir in the mascarpone and melted chocolate.

2 Mix the sweetened coffee and rum or brandy together in a bowl. Dip the sponge fingers into the mixture briefly so that they absorb the coffee mixture but do not become soggy.

3 Place 3 sponge fingers on each of 4 serving plates.

4 Spoon a layer of the mascarpone and chocolate mixture over the sponge fingers.

5 Place 3 more sponge fingers on top of the mascarpone layer. Spread another layer of mascarpone and chocolate mixture and place 3 more sponge fingers on top.

6 Leave the tiramisu to chill in the refrigerator for at least 1 hour. Dust all over with a little cocoa powder just before serving.

🍮 COOK'S TIP

For a nutty taste, try adding 50 g/1¾ oz toasted chopped hazelnuts to the chocolate cream mixture in Step 1.

⭐⭐   easy

1 hr 25 mins

5 mins

Another rich chocolate dessert, this loaf is very simple to make and can be served as a tea-time treat as well.

Rich Chocolate Loaf

1 Line a 675-g/1½-lb loaf tin with a sheet of kitchen foil.

2 Place the chocolate, butter, condensed milk and cinnamon in a heavy-based saucepan. Heat gently, stirring, until melted and smoothly combined.

3 Stir the almonds, biscuits and apricots into the chocolate mixture until thoroughly coated.

4 Pour the mixture into the prepared tin and leave to chill in the refrigerator for about 1 hour or until set.

5 The loaf is very rich, so cut it into thin slices to serve.

MAKES 16 SLICES

150 g/5½ oz dark chocolate
6 tbsp unsalted butter
210 ml/7¼ fl oz condensed milk
2 tsp cinnamon
75 g/2¾ oz almonds, chopped roughly
75 g/2¾ oz amaretti biscuits, broken
50 g/1¾ oz ready-to-eat dried apricots, chopped roughly

COOK'S TIP

This simple but luxurious recipe can be adapted endlessly, according to your taste or what is available in your store cupboard.

very easy

1 hr 20 mins

5 mins

This is a light and fluffy mousse with a subtle hint of orange. It is wickedly delicious served with a fresh fruit sauce.

Chocolate Mousse

SERVES 8

100 g/3½ oz dark chocolate, melted
300 ml/10 fl oz natural yogurt
150 ml/5 fl oz low-fat soft cheese
4 tbsp caster sugar
1 tbsp orange juice
1 tbsp brandy
1½ tsp vegetarian gelatine
9 tbsp cold water
2 large egg whites

to decorate
roughly grated dark and white chocolate
orange rind

1 Put the melted chocolate, yogurt, soft cheese, sugar, orange juice and brandy in a food processor or blender and process for 30 seconds. Transfer the mixture to a large bowl.

2 Sprinkle the vegetarian gelatine over the water and stir until dissolved.

3 In a pan, bring the vegetarian gelatine and water to the boil and boil for 2 minutes. Cool slightly, then stir into the chocolate.

4 Whisk the egg whites until stiff peaks form and fold into the chocolate mixture using a metal spoon.

5 Line a 500-g/1-lb 2 oz loaf tin with clingfilm. Spoon the mousse into the tin. Chill in the refrigerator for 2 hours, until set. Turn the mousse out on to a serving plate, decorate and serve.

easy

2 hrs 15 mins

5 mins

COOK'S TIP

For a quick mandarin sauce to serve with the mousse, process a can of mandarin segments in natural juice in a food processor and press through a sieve. Sweeten with 1 tablespoon clear honey.

This dairy-free cheesecake is easy to prepare and lower in fat than most traditional cheesecakes.

Chocolate Tofu Cheesecake

1 Put the flour, ground almonds and 1 tablespoon of the sugar in a bowl and mix well. Rub the margarine into the mixture and form into a dough.

2 Lightly grease and line the base of a 23-cm/9-inch springform tin. Press the dough into the base of the tin, pushing it right up to the edges.

3 Roughly chop the tofu and put in a food processor with the vegetable oil, orange juice, brandy, cocoa powder, almond essence and remaining sugar. Process until smooth and creamy. Pour over the base in the tin and cook in a preheated oven, 160°C/325°F/Gas Mark 3, for 1–1¼ hours or until set.

4 Leave to cool in the tin for 5 minutes, then remove from the tin and chill in the refrigerator. Dust with icing sugar and cocoa powder. Decorate with Cape gooseberries and serve.

SERVES 12

100 g/3½ oz plain flour, sifted
100 g/3½ oz ground almonds
200 g/7 oz dark muscovado sugar
150 g/5½ oz margarine
675 g/1 lb 8 oz firm tofu
175 ml/6 fl oz vegetable oil
125 ml/4 fl oz orange juice
175 ml/6 fl oz brandy
6 tbsp cocoa powder
2 tsp almond essence

to decorate
icing sugar
cocoa powder
Cape gooseberries

 COOK'S TIP

Cape gooseberries make an attractive decoration for many desserts. Peel open the papery husks to expose the bright orange fruits.

★★   easy
      15 mins
      1 hr–1 hr 15 mins

A combination of feather-light chocolate and coffee mousses, swirled together in their serving glasses.

Mocha Swirl Mousse

SERVES 4

1 tbsp coffee and chicory essence
2 tsp cocoa powder, plus extra for dusting
1 tsp low-fat drinking chocolate powder
150 ml/5 fl oz low-fat crème fraîche, plus 4 tsp to serve
2 tsp powdered gelatine
2 tbsp water
2 large egg whites
2 tbsp caster sugar
4 chocolate coffee beans, to serve

1 Place the coffee and chicory essence in one bowl, and 2 teaspoons cocoa powder and the drinking chocolate in another bowl. Divide the crème fraîche between the 2 bowls and mix both well.

2 Sprinkle the gelatine over the water in a heatproof bowl and leave to go spongy. Place over a pan of hot water and stir until dissolved. In a clean bowl, whisk the egg whites and sugar until stiff and divide this evenly between the 2 mixtures.

3 Divide the dissolved gelatine between the 2 mixtures and, using a large metal spoon, gently fold in until well mixed.

4 Spoon small amounts of the 2 mousses alternately into 4 serving glasses and swirl together gently. Chill for 1 hour or until set.

5 To serve, top each mousse with a teaspoonful of crème fraîche, a chocolate coffee bean and a light dusting of cocoa powder. Serve immediately.

easy

1 hr 15 mins

0 mins

🍴 **COOK'S TIP**

For vegetarians, instead of gelatine use a vegetarian equivalent, available from health-food shops. However, be sure to read the instructions on the packet first as it is prepared differently from normal gelatine.

This famous Tuscan honey and nut cake is a Christmas speciality. In Italy it is sold in pretty boxes, and served in very thin slices.

Panforte *di* Siena

1 Toast the almonds under the grill until lightly browned and place in a bowl.

2 Toast the hazelnuts until the skins split. Place on a dry tea towel and rub off the skins. Roughly chop the hazelnuts and add them to the almonds with the mixed peel.

3 Chop the apricots and pineapple fairly finely, add to the nuts with the orange rind and mix well.

4 Sift the flour with the cocoa and cinnamon, add to the nut mixture and stir well to combine.

5 Line a 20-cm/8-inch round cake tin or deep loose-bottomed flan tin with baking paper.

6 Put the sugar and honey into a saucepan and heat until the sugar dissolves, then boil gently for about 5 minutes or until the mixture thickens and begins to turn a deeper shade of brown. Quickly add it to the nut mixture and mix together evenly. Turn into the prepared tin and level the top using the back of a damp spoon.

7 Cook in a preheated oven, 150°C/300°F/Gas Mark 2, for 1 hour. Remove from the oven and leave in the tin until cold. Take out of the tin and carefully peel off the paper. Before serving, dredge the cake heavily with sifted icing sugar. Serve in thin slices.

SERVES 12

125 g/4½ oz split whole almonds
125 g/4½ oz hazelnuts
85 g/3 oz chopped mixed peel
55 g/2 oz ready-to-eat dried apricots
55 g/2 oz glacé or crystallized pineapple
grated rind of 1 large orange
6 tbsp plain flour
2 tbsp cocoa powder
2 tsp ground cinnamon
125 g/4½ oz caster sugar
175 g/6 oz honey
icing sugar, for dredging

moderate

10 mins

1 hr 15 mins

Rich, creamy gelati, or ice creams, are one of the great Italian culinary contributions to the world. This version is made with fresh mint.

Mint-chocolate Gelato

SERVES 4

6 large eggs
150 g/5½ oz caster sugar
300 ml/10 fl oz milk
150 ml/5 fl oz double cream
large handful fresh mint leaves, rinsed
    and dried
2 drops green food colouring, optional
55 g/2 oz dark chocolate, chopped finely

1 Put the eggs and sugar in a heatproof bowl that will sit over a saucepan with plenty of room underneath. Using an electric mixer, beat the eggs and sugar together until thick and creamy.

2 Put the milk and cream in the saucepan and bring to a simmer, stirring. Pour on to the eggs, whisking constantly.

3 Rinse the pan and put 2.5 cm/1 inch of water in the bottom. Place the bowl on top, making sure the base does not touch the water. Turn the heat to medium–high and stir the custard over the hot water until it is thick enough to coat the back of the spoon and, your finger leaves mark when you pull it across the spoon.

4 Tear the mint leaves and stir them into the custard. Remove the custard from the heat. Leave to cool, then cover and infuse for at least 2 hours, chilling for the last 30 minutes.

5 Strain the mixture through a small nylon sieve to remove the pieces of mint. Stir in the food colouring, if using. Transfer to a freezer-proof container and freeze the mixture for 1–2 hours until frozen 2.5 cm/1 inch from the sides.

6 Scrape into a bowl and beat again until smooth. Stir in the chocolate pieces, smooth the top, cover with clingfilm or kitchen foil and freeze until it is set. Store frozen for up to 3 months. Soften the ice cream in the refrigerator for 20 minutes before serving.

moderate

5–6 hrs

20 mins

Richly flavoured and with a wonderful texture, this home-made ice cream really couldn't be simpler.

Marshmallow Ice Cream

1 Put the chocolate and marshmallows in a pan and pour in the milk. Warm over a very low heat until the chocolate and marshmallows have melted. Remove from the heat and leave the mixture to cool completely.

2 Whisk the cream until thick, then fold it into the cold chocolate mixture with a metal spoon. Pour into a 450-g/ 1-lb loaf tin and freeze for at least 2 hours, until firm (it will keep for 1 month in the freezer).

SERVES 4

85 g/3 oz dark chocolate, broken into pieces
175 g/6 oz white marshmallows
150 ml/5 fl oz milk
300 ml/10 fl oz double cream

👨‍🍳 COOK'S TIP

As a variation, you could make half of the mixture with dark chocolate and half with white chocolate, and swirl the 2 mixtures together in the tin before freezing.

⭐ very easy

🕐 2 hrs 40 mins

🕐 5–10 mins

This is a truly special sorbet and it is worth buying the best possible quality chocolate for it.

Chocolate Sorbet

SERVES 6

140 g/5 oz continental chocolate, chopped roughly
140 g/5 oz dark chocolate, chopped roughly
475 ml/16 fl oz water
200 g/7 oz caster sugar
langues de chats biscuits, to serve

1 Put both types of chocolate into a food processor and process briefly until very finely chopped.

2 Pour the water into a heavy-based pan and add the sugar. Stir over a medium heat to dissolve, then bring to the boil. Boil for 2 minutes, without stirring, then remove the pan from the heat.

3 With the motor of the food processor running, pour the hot syrup on to the chocolate. Process for about 2 minutes, until all the chocolate has melted and the mixture is smooth. Scrape down the sides of the food processor, if necessary. Strain the chocolate mixture into a freezer-proof container and leave to cool.

4 When the mixture is cool, place it in the freezer for about 1 hour, until slushy, but beginning to become firm around the edges. Tip the mixture into the food processor and process until smooth. Return to the container and freeze for at least 2 hours until firm.

5 Remove the sorbet from the freezer about 10 minutes before serving and let it stand at room temperature to allow it to soften slightly. Serve in scoops with langues de chats biscuits.

★★   easy
3 hrs 10 mins
10 mins

What could be more delicious than creamy, tender rice cooked in a rich chocolate sauce? This dessert is almost like a dense chocolate mousse.

Chocolate Rice Dessert

1 Bring a saucepan of water to the boil. Sprinkle in the rice and add the salt. Reduce the heat and simmer gently for 15–20 minutes, until the rice is just tender. Drain, rinse and drain again.

2 Heat the milk and the sugar in a large, heavy-based saucepan over a medium heat until the sugar dissolves, stirring frequently. Add the chocolate and butter and stir until melted and smooth.

3 Stir in the cooked rice and reduce the heat to low. Cover and simmer, stirring occasionally, for 30 minutes, until the milk is absorbed and the mixture thickened. Stir in the vanilla essence and brandy. Remove from the heat and allow to cool to room temperature.

4 Whisk the cream until soft peaks form. Stir one heaped spoonful of the cream into the chocolate rice mixture to lighten it, then fold in the remaining cream.

5 Spoon into glass serving dishes, cover and chill for about 2 hours. If wished, decorate with whipped cream and top with Quick Curls.

SERVES **8**

100 g/3½ oz long-grain white rice
pinch of salt
600 ml/1 pint milk
100 g/3½ oz granulated sugar
200 g/7 oz continental or dark chocolate, chopped
5 tbsp butter, diced
1 tsp vanilla essence
2 tbsp brandy
175 ml/6 fl oz double cream
whipped cream, for piping (optional)
Quick Curls (see page 15), to decorate (optional)

🍥 **COOK'S TIP**

To mould the chocolate rice, soften 1 sachet of gelatine in about 50 ml/2¼ fl oz cold water and heat gently until dissolved. Stir into the chocolate just before folding in the cream. Pour into a rinsed mould, allow to set, then unmould.

easy
2 hrs 5 mins
1 hr 10 mins

The slight tartness of satsumas beautifully counterbalances the richness of this delicious and unusual trifle.

Chocolate *and* Orange Trifle

SERVES 6

4 trifle sponges
2 large chocolate coconut
    macaroons, crumbled
4 tbsp sweet sherry
8 satsumas
2 egg yolks
2 tbsp caster sugar
2 tbsp cornflour
200 ml/7 fl oz milk
250 g/9 oz mascarpone cheese
200 g/7 oz dark chocolate, melted
225 ml/7½ fl oz double cream

to decorate
marbled chocolate shapes (see Cook's Tip)
10–12 satsuma segments

1 Break up the trifle sponges and place them in a large glass serving dish. Sprinkle the crumbled macaroons on top, then sprinkle with the sherry. Squeeze the juice from two of the satsumas and sprinkle it over the crumbled macaroons. Peel and segment the remaining satsumas and arrange them in the dish.

2 In a large bowl, mix together the egg yolks, sugar and cornflour to make a smooth paste. Bring the milk to just below boiling point in a small pan. Remove from the heat and pour it into the egg yolk mixture, stirring constantly. Return the custard to a clean pan and cook over a low heat, stirring constantly, until thickened and smooth.

3 Return the custard to the bowl, then stir in the mascarpone and melted chocolate until thoroughly combined. Spread the chocolate custard evenly over the trifle base and chill in the refrigerator for 1 hour, until set.

4 Whip the cream until thick, then spread it over the top of the trifle. Decorate with marbled chocolate shapes and satsuma segments.

easy

1 hr 25 mins

15–20 mins

🍴 **COOK'S TIP**

To make marbled chocolate shapes, spread melted dark chocolate on a piece of baking paper and immediately pipe a fine scribble of melted white chocolate over it. Marble with a cocktail stick. When firm but not hard, cut into shapes.

Sweet strawberries are teamed with rich and creamy mascarpone cheese and luxurious white chocolate to make this stunning cheesecake.

Strawberry Cheesecake

1 To make the base, melt the butter in a saucepan over a low heat and stir in the crushed biscuits and the nuts. Spoon the mixture into a 23-cm/9-inch loose-bottomed cake tin and press evenly over the base with the back of a spoon. Set aside.

2 To make the filling, beat the cheese until smooth, then beat in the eggs and sugar. Stir in the melted chocolate and finally the strawberries.

3 Spoon the mixture into the cake tin, spread out evenly and smooth the surface. Bake in a preheated oven, 150°C/300°F/Gas Mark 2, for 1 hour, until the filling is just firm. Turn off the oven but leave the cheesecake in it until completely cold.

4 Transfer the cheesecake to a serving plate and spread the mascarpone on top. Decorate with chocolate caraque and whole strawberries.

SERVES **8**

base
4 tbsp unsalted butter
225 g/8 oz digestive biscuits, crushed
55 g/2 oz chopped walnuts

filling
450 g/1 lb mascarpone cheese
2 eggs, beaten
3 tbsp caster sugar
250 g/9 oz white chocolate, melted
225 g/8 oz strawberries, hulled
   and quartered

topping
175 g/6 oz mascarpone cheese
chocolate Caraque (see page 15)
16 whole strawberries

easy
3 hrs
1 hr

CHOCOLATE

This classic American dessert is packed with deliciously contrasting flavours and textures and is simply irresistible.

Chocolate Pecan Pie

MAKES A 25-CM/10-INCH PIE

pastry
280 g/10 oz plain flour, plus flour for dusting
6 tbsp cocoa powder
115 g/4 oz icing sugar
pinch of salt
200 g/7 oz unsalted butter, diced
1 egg yolk

filling
350 g/12 oz shelled pecan nuts
6 tbsp unsalted butter
175 g/6 oz brown sugar
3 eggs
2 tbsp double cream
2 tbsp plain flour
85 g/3 oz dark chocolate, melted
1 tbsp icing sugar, to dust

moderate
2 hrs 40 mins
1 hr 15 mins

1 To make the pastry, sift the flour, cocoa, sugar and salt into a mixing bowl and make a well in the centre. Put the butter and egg yolk in the well and knead together, then gradually mix in the dry ingredients. Knead lightly into a ball. Cover with clingfilm and chill in the refrigerator for 1 hour.

2 Unwrap the dough and roll it out on a lightly floured surface. Use it to line a 25-cm/10-inch non-stick springform pie tin and prick the base with a fork. Line the pastry case with baking paper and fill with baking beans. Bake in a preheated oven, 180°C/350°F/Gas Mark 4, for 15 minutes. Remove from the oven, discard the beans and paper, and let it cool. Leave the oven switched on.

3 Roughly chop 225 g/8 oz of the pecans. Mix the butter with 55 g/2 oz of the brown sugar. Beat in the eggs, one at a time, then add the remaining brown sugar and mix well. Stir in the double cream, flour, melted chocolate and chopped pecans.

4 Spoon the filling into the pastry case and smooth the surface. Cut the remaining pecans in half and arrange in concentric circles over the pie.

5 Bake in the preheated oven for 30 minutes, then cover the top of the pie with foil to prevent it from burning and bake for a further 25 minutes. Remove the pie from the oven and let it cool slightly before removing from the tin and transferring to a wire rack to cool completely. Dust with icing sugar before serving.

This is a family favourite –
spiral slices of sponge cake
and ice cream never fail
to please.

Chocolate Ice Cream Roll

1 Line a 38 x 25-cm/15 x 10-inch Swiss roll tin with greaseproof paper. Grease
the base and dust with flour. Put the eggs and caster sugar into the top of a
double boiler or in a heatproof bowl set over a pan of barely simmering
water. Beat over a low heat for 5–10 minutes until the mixture is pale and
fluffy. Remove from the heat and continue beating for 10 minutes, until the
mixture is cool and the whisk leaves a ribbon trail when lifted. Sift the flour
and cocoa powder over the surface and gently fold it in.

2 Pour the mixture into the prepared tin and spread evenly with a palette
knife. Bake in a preheated oven, 190°C/375°F/Gas Mark 5, for 15 minutes, until
firm to the touch and beginning to shrink from the sides of the tin.

3 Spread out a clean tea towel and cover with a sheet of baking paper. Lightly
dust the paper with icing sugar. Turn out the cake on to the baking paper and
carefully peel off the lining paper. Trim off any crusty edges. Starting from a
short side, pick up the cake and the baking paper and roll them up together.
Wrap the tea towel around the rolled cake and place on a wire rack to cool.

4 Put the frozen ice cream in the refrigerator for 15–20 minutes to soften
slightly. Unroll the cake and spread it evenly with the ice cream. Roll it up
again without the baking paper. Wrap in foil and freeze until firm.

5 Transfer the cake from the freezer to the refrigerator about 20 minutes
before serving. Unwrap, place on a serving plate and dust with icing sugar.
Arrange the quick curls on top. Serve in slices with white chocolate
fudge sauce.

SERVES 8

115 g/4 oz plain flour, plus flour for dusting
4 eggs
115 g/4 oz caster sugar
115 g/4 oz plain flour
3 tbsp cocoa powder
icing sugar, to dust
600 ml/1 pint chocolate ice cream
Quick Curls, to decorate (see page 15)
225 ml/8 fl oz White Chocolate Fudge Sauce ,
  to serve (see page 73)

✪✪✪   moderate
1 hr 15 mins
20–25 mins

This richly flavoured flan looks superb and tastes simply wonderful – a perfect choice for a special occasion dessert.

Blackberry Chocolate Flan

S E R V E S 6

280 g/10 oz plain flour, plus flour for dusting
55 g/2 oz cocoa powder
115 g/4 oz icing sugar
pinch of salt
200 g/7 oz unsalted butter, diced
1 egg yolk

filling

300 ml/10 fl oz double cream
175 g/6 oz blackberry jam
225 g/8 oz dark chocolate, broken into pieces
55 g/2 oz unsalted butter, diced

sauce

675 g/1 lb 8 oz blackberries
1 tbsp lemon juice
2 tbsp caster sugar
2 tbsp crème de cassis

moderate

2 hrs 30 mins

15 mins

1 First, make the pastry. Sift the flour, cocoa, icing sugar and a pinch of salt into a mixing bowl and make a well in the centre. Put the butter and egg yolk in the well and gradually mix in the dry ingredients, using a pastry blender or two forks. Knead lightly and form into a ball. Cover with clingfilm and chill in the refrigerator for 1 hour.

2 Roll the dough out on a lightly floured surface and use it to line a 30 x 10-cm/12 x 4-inch rectangular flan tin and prick the base with a fork. Line the pastry case with baking paper and fill with baking beans. Bake in a preheated oven, 180°C/350°F/Gas Mark 4, for 15 minutes. Remove from the oven, remove the beans and paper and set aside to cool.

3 To make the filling, put the cream and jam into a pan and bring to the boil over a low heat. Remove the pan from the heat and stir in the chocolate and butter until melted and smooth. Pour the mixture into the pastry case and set aside to cool.

4 To make the sauce, put 225 g/8 oz of the blackberries, the lemon juice and caster sugar into a food processor and process until smooth. Transfer to a bowl and stir in the crème de cassis.

5 Remove the flan from the tin and place on a serving plate. Arrange the remaining blackberries on top and brush with a little of the blackberry sauce. Serve the flan and hand the sauce separately.

This famous Italian cream bombe is named *Zuccotto* because its shape resembles a pumpkin, or *zucca*.

Zuccotto

1 In a large bowl, whisk the cream until it is stiff, then fold in the sugar, followed by the hazelnuts, cherries and chocolate. Cover with clingfilm and chill in the refrigerator until required.

2 Meanwhile, cut the cakes in half horizontally and then cut the pieces to line the base and sides of a 1.25-litre/2-pint pudding basin. Reserve the remaining sponge cake. Mix together the brandy and amaretto and sprinkle over the sponge cake lining.

3 Remove the cream filling from the refrigerator and spoon it into the lined basin. Cover the top with the remaining sponge cake, cut to fit. Cover with clingfilm and chill in the refrigerator for at least 2 hours.

4 To serve, remove the zuccotto from the refrigerator and run a round-bladed knife around the sides to loosen it. Place a serving plate on top of the basin and, holding them firmly together, invert. Dust two opposite quarters of the zuccotto with icing sugar and the other opposite quarters with cocoa to make alternating sections of colour.

SERVES 8

600 ml/1 pint double cream
2 tbsp icing sugar
55 g/2 oz hazelnuts, toasted
225 g/8 oz cherries, halved and stoned
115 g/4 oz dark chocolate, chopped finely
2 x 20-cm/8-inch round chocolate
   sponge cakes
4 tbsp brandy
4 tbsp amaretto liqueur

to decorate
2 tbsp icing sugar, sifted
2 tbsp cocoa powder, sifted

🍳 **COOK'S TIP**

Substitute almonds for the hazelnuts and a mixture of glacé cherries and candied peel for the fresh cherries, if you like.

 moderate

🕐 2 hrs 30 mins

🕐 0 mins

Contrasting flavours, textures and colours are combined to create this delectable masterpiece.

Chocolate *and* Orange Slices

S E R V E S 8

2 tsp butter, for greasing
450 g/1 lb dark chocolate, broken into pieces
3 small, loose-skinned oranges, such as tangerines, mandarins or satsumas
4 egg yolks
200 ml/7 fl oz crème fraîche
2 tbsp raisins
300 ml/10 fl oz whipped cream, to serve

1 Grease a 450-g/1-lb loaf tin and line it with clingfilm. Melt 400 g/14 oz of the chocolate and cool slightly.

2 Meanwhile, peel the oranges, removing all traces of pith. Cut the rind into matchsticks. Beat the egg yolks into the chocolate, one at a time, then add most of the orange rind (reserve the rest for decoration), and all the crème fraîche and raisins and beat until smooth and thoroughly combined. Spoon the mixture into the prepared tin, cover with clingfilm and chill in the refrigerator for 3–4 hours, until set.

3 Meanwhile, melt the remaining chocolate. Segment the oranges. Dip each segment into the melted chocolate and spread out on a sheet of baking paper for about 30 minutes, until set.

4 To serve, remove the tin from the refrigerator and turn out the chocolate mould. Remove the clingfilm and cut the mould into slices. Place a slice on each of 8 individual serving plates and decorate with the chocolate-coated orange segments and the remaining orange rind. Serve immediately, with whipped cream.

moderate
4 hrs 40 mins
10 mins

🍳 COOK'S TIP

Take care to remove all traces of pith from the orange rind, as it tastes bitter and has a fibrous texture.

Don't be alarmed – this rich Italian dessert gets its name from its appearance, and not from its ingredients.

Chocolate Salami

1 Put the chocolate in the top of a double boiler or in a heatproof bowl set over a pan of barely simmering water. Add the liqueur or brandy and about 2 tablespoons of the butter. Stir over a low heat until melted and smooth. Remove from the heat and cool slightly.

2 Stir in the egg yolks, then stir in the remaining butter, a little at a time, making sure each addition is fully incorporated before adding more. Stir in about three-quarters of the crushed biscuits and all the toasted almonds. Cover with clingfilm then set aside for 45–60 minutes, until beginning to set. Meanwhile, put the remaining crushed biscuits in a food processor and process until finely crushed. Transfer them to a bowl and stir in the ground almonds, then set aside.

3 Lightly oil a sheet of baking paper and turn out the chocolate mixture on to it. Using a palette knife, shape the mixture into a salami about 35 cm/14 inches long. Wrap the salami in the paper and place in the freezer for 4–6 hours, until set.

4 About 1¼ hours before serving, spread out the ground almond mixture on a sheet of baking paper. Remove the salami from the freezer and unwrap. Roll it over the ground almond mixture until thoroughly and evenly coated. Cover with clingfilm then set aside for 1 hour at room temperature. Cut into slices and serve.

SERVES 10

350 g/12 oz dark chocolate, broken into small pieces
4 tbsp amaretto liqueur or brandy
225 g/8 oz unsalted butter, cut into small pieces
2 egg yolks
24 plain sweet biscuits, such as Petit Beurre, crushed roughly
55 g/2 oz toasted flaked almonds, chopped
25 g/1 oz ground almonds

★★★   moderate

6 hrs 25 mins

5 mins

CHOCOLATE

Green and black grapes
decorate the creamy
chocolate filling in these
crisp little pastry nests.

Filo Nests

SERVES 4

1 tbsp unsalted butter
6 sheets filo pastry, each about 30 x 15 cm/
   12 x 6 inches
40 g/1½ oz dark chocolate, melted
115 g/4 oz ricotta cheese
16 seedless green grapes, halved
24 seedless black grapes, halved

1 Put the butter into a small pan and set over a low heat until melted. Remove from the heat. Cut each sheet of pastry into four, to give 24 rectangles, each measuring about 15 x 7.5 cm/6 x 3 inches, then stack them all on top of each other. Brush 4 shallow tartlet tins with melted butter. Line 1 tin with a rectangle of pastry, brush with melted butter, and place another rectangle on top at an angle to the first and brush it with melted butter. Continue in this way, lining each tin with 6 rectangles, each brushed with melted butter. Brush the top layers with melted butter.

2 Bake in a preheated oven, 190°C/375°F/Gas Mark 5, for 7–8 minutes, until golden and crisp. Remove from the oven and set aside to cool in the tins.

3 Brush the insides of the pastry cases with about half the melted chocolate. Beat the ricotta in a small bowl until smooth, then beat in the remaining melted chocolate.

4 Divide the chocolate ricotta between the pastry cases and arrange the grapes alternately around the edges. Carefully lift the pastry cases out of the tins and serve immediately.

moderate

45 mins

15–20 mins

This unusual combination of flavours makes a sophisticated and tempting dessert to serve at a dinner party.

Chocolate *and* Pernod Creams

1 Put the chocolate in the top of a double boiler or in a heatproof bowl set over a pan of barely simmering water. Stir over a low heat until melted. Remove the pan from the heat and cool slightly.

2 Pour the milk and cream into a pan over a low heat and bring to just below boiling point, stirring occasionally. Remove the pan from the heat and then set aside.

3 Beat the sugar and the arrowroot mixture into the melted chocolate. Gradually stir in the hot milk and cream mixture, then stir in the Pernod. Return the double boiler to the heat or set the bowl over a pan of barely simmering water and cook over a low heat for about 10 minutes, stirring constantly, until thick and smooth. Remove from the heat and then set aside to cool.

4 Pour the chocolate and Pernod mixture into 4 individual serving glasses. Cover with clingfilm and chill in the refrigerator for 2 hours before serving with langues de chats biscuits or chocolate-tipped rolled wafers.

SERVES 4

55 g/2 oz dark chocolate, broken into pieces
250 ml/8 fl oz milk
300 ml/10 fl oz double cream
2 tbsp caster sugar
1 tbsp arrowroot mixed with 2 tbsp milk
3 tbsp Pernod
langues de chats biscuits, or chocolate-tipped rolled wafers, to serve

🍴 COOK'S TIP

Arrowroot is used rather than cornflour to thicken this delicate dessert as it becomes clear and completely flavourless when cooked.

⭐⭐   easy
🕐   2 hrs 10 mins
🕐   20 mins

This pretty, colourful dessert is deliciously refreshing and would make a good finale to an *al fresco* meal.

White Chocolate Moulds

S E R V E S 8

250 ml/8 fl oz double cream
3 tbsp crème fraîche
125 g/4½ oz white chocolate, melted
2 eggs, separated
3 tbsp water
1½ tsp gelatine
vegetable oil, for greasing
140 g/5 oz sliced strawberries
140 g/5 oz raspberries
140 g/5 oz blackcurrants
5 tbsp caster sugar
125 ml/4 fl oz crème de framboise
12 blackcurrant leaves (if available)

1 Pour the cream into a pan and bring to just below boiling point over a low heat. Remove from the heat, then stir in the crème fraîche and melted chocolate. Leave to cool slightly, then beat in the egg yolks, one at a time.

2 Pour the water into a small, heatproof bowl and sprinkle the gelatine on the surface. Leave for 2–3 minutes, until spongy, then set over a pan of barely simmering water until completely dissolved. Stir the gelatine into the chocolate mixture and then leave until nearly set.

3 Brush the inside of 6 timbales, ramekins, dariole moulds or small cups with oil and line the bases with baking paper. Whisk the egg whites until soft peaks form, then fold them into the chocolate mixture. Divide the mixture evenly among the prepared moulds and smooth the surface. Cover with clingfilm and chill in the refrigerator for 2 hours, until set.

4 Put the strawberries, raspberries and blackcurrants in a bowl and sprinkle with the caster sugar. Pour in the liqueur and stir gently to mix. Cover with clingfilm and then chill in the refrigerator for 2 hours.

5 To serve, run a round-bladed knife around the sides of the moulds and turn out on to individual serving plates. Divide the fruit among the plates and serve immediately, garnished with blackcurrant leaves, if available.

✪✪✪ moderate

3 hrs 20 mins

15 mins

Richly flavoured moulded ice creams make a scrumptious summertime dessert for all the family.

Chocolate *and* Hazelnut Parfait

1 Spread the hazelnuts on a baking tray and toast under a grill preheated to medium, shaking the tray from time to time for about 5 minutes, until golden all over. Set aside to cool.

2 Process the cooled toasted hazelnuts in a food processor until finely ground.

3 Whisk the cream until it is stiff, then fold in the ground hazelnuts and set aside. In a large bowl, whisk the egg yolks with 3 tablespoons of the sugar for 10 minutes, until pale and thick.

4 Whisk the egg whites in a separate bowl until soft peaks form. Whisk in the remaining sugar, a little at a time, until the whites are stiff and glossy. Stir the cooled melted chocolate into the egg yolk mixture, then fold in the cream and then the egg whites. Divide the mixture among 6 freezerproof timbales or moulds, cover with clingfilm and freeze for at least 8 hours or overnight, until firm.

5 Transfer the parfaits to the refrigerator about 10 minutes before serving to soften slightly. Turn out on to individual serving plates, dust the tops lightly with cocoa, decorate with mint sprigs and serve with wafers.

SERVES 6

175 g/6 oz blanched hazelnuts
600 ml/1 pint double cream
3 eggs, separated
250 g/9 oz icing sugar, sifted
175 g/6 oz dark chocolate, melted and cooled
1 tbsp cocoa powder, to dust
6 small fresh mint sprigs, to decorate
wafer biscuits, to serve

COOK'S TIP

Keep a sharp eye on nuts toasting under the grill, as they can burn very quickly and easily

moderate
8 hrs 30 mins
10 mins

Ice cream is always a popular summer dessert – try this rather different recipe for a change.

Chocolate *and* Honey Ice Cream

SERVES 8

500 ml/18 fl oz milk
200 g/7 oz dark chocolate, broken
   into pieces
4 eggs, separated
85 g/3 oz caster sugar
pinch of salt
2 tbsp clear honey
12 fresh strawberries, washed, to decorate

1 Pour the milk into a pan, add 150 g/5½ oz of the chocolate and stir over a medium heat for 3–5 minutes, until melted. Remove the pan from the heat and set aside.

2 In a separate bowl, whisk the egg yolks with all but 1 tablespoon of the sugar until pale and thickened. Gradually whisk in the milk mixture, a little at a time. Return the mixture to a clean pan and cook over a low heat, whisking constantly, until smooth and thickened. Remove from the heat and set aside to cool completely. Cover with clingfilm and chill in the refrigerator for 30 minutes.

3 Whisk the egg whites with a pinch of salt until soft peaks form. Gradually whisk in the remaining sugar and continue whisking until stiff and glossy. Remove the chocolate mixture from the refrigerator and stir in the honey, then gently fold in the egg whites.

4 Divide the mixture among 6 individual freezerproof moulds and place in the freezer for at least 4 hours, until frozen. Meanwhile, put the remaining chocolate in the top of a double boiler or in a heatproof bowl set over a pan of barely simmering water. Stir over a low heat until melted and smooth, then dip the strawberries in the melted chocolate so that they are half-coated. Leave to set on a sheet of baking paper. Transfer the ice cream to the refrigerator for 10 minutes before serving. Turn out onto serving plates and decorate with the strawberries.

moderate

5 hrs 30 mins

15 mins

The nutty crust of this delectable American pie contrasts with the tempting creamy chocolate filling.

Chocolate Chiffon Pie

1 Put the Brazil nuts into a food processor and process until finely ground. Add the granulated sugar and melted butter and process briefly to combine. Tip the mixture into a 23-cm/9-inch round pie tin or dish and press it on to the base and sides with a spoon or your fingertips. Bake in a preheated oven, 200°C/400°F/Gas Mark 6, for 8–10 minutes, until light golden brown. Set aside to cool.

2 Pour the milk into the top of a double boiler or into a heatproof bowl and sprinkle the gelatine over the surface. Allow to soften for 2 minutes, then place over a pan of barely simmering water. Stir in half the caster sugar, both the egg yolks and all the chocolate. Stir constantly over a low heat for 4–5 minutes, until the gelatine has dissolved and the chocolate has melted. Remove from the heat and beat until the mixture is smooth and thoroughly blended. Stir in the vanilla essence, cover with clingfilm and chill in the refrigerator for 45–60 minutes, until just beginning to set.

3 Whip the cream until it is stiff, then fold all but about 3 tablespoons into the chocolate mixture. Whisk the egg whites in another bowl until soft peaks form. Add 2 teaspoons of the remaining sugar and whisk until stiff peaks form. Fold in the remaining sugar, then fold the egg whites into the chocolate mixture. Pour the filling into the pie dish and chill in the refrigerator for 3 hours, or until set. Decorate the pie with the remaining whipped cream and the chopped nuts before serving.

SERVES **8**

140 g/5 oz shelled Brazil nuts
2 tbsp granulated sugar
2 tsp melted butter
250 ml/8 fl oz milk
2 tsp gelatine
115 g/4 oz caster sugar
2 eggs, separated
225 g/8 oz dark chocolate, chopped roughly
1 tsp vanilla essence
150 ml/5 fl oz double cream
2 tbsp chopped Brazil nuts

✪✪✪   moderate

🕐   5 hrs 5 mins

🕐   15 mins

Small Cakes *and* Cookies

This chapter contains everyday delights for chocolate fans. You are sure to be tempted by our wonderful array of cookies and small cakes. Make any day special with a home-made chocolate biscuit to be served with coffee, as a snack or to accompany a special dessert. Although some take a little longer to make, most are quick and easy to prepare and decoration is often simple although you can get carried away if you like!

You'll find recipes for old favourites such as Chocolate Chip Muffins and Chocolate Chip Cookies, Chocolate Cup Cakes and Sticky Chocolate Brownies. There are also new biscuits and small cakes, such as Chocolate Coconut Squares or Chocolate Pretzels. Finally, we have given the chocolate treatment to some traditional recipes – try Chocolate Scones or Chocolate Chip Flapjacks.

A variation on an old favourite, both kids and grown-ups will love these scrumptious little cakes.

Chocolate Cup Cakes

MAKES 18

100 g/3½ oz butter, softened
100 g/3½ oz caster sugar
2 eggs, beaten lightly
150 g/5½ oz self-raising flour
2 tbsp milk
50 g/1¾ oz dark chocolate chips
2 tbsp cocoa powder

white chocolate icing
150 g/5½ oz low-fat soft cheese
225 g/8 oz white chocolate, melted
   and cooled

1 Line an 18-hole bun tray with individual paper cup cases.

2 Beat together the butter and sugar until pale and fluffy. Gradually add the eggs, beating well after each addition. Add a little of the flour if the mixture begins to curdle. Add the milk, then fold in the chocolate chips.

3 Sift together the flour and cocoa powder and fold into the mixture with a metal spoon or spatula. Divide the mixture equally between the paper cases and level the tops.

4 Bake in a preheated oven, 180°C/350°F/Gas Mark 4, for 20 minutes or until well risen and springy to the touch. Leave to cool on a wire rack.

5 To make the icing, beat the cheese until softened slightly, then beat in the melted chocolate. Spread a little of the icing over each cup cake and chill for 1 hour before serving.

⭐⭐   easy
🌓   1 hr 15 mins
🕐   20 mins

🍴 **COOK'S TIP**

Add white chocolate chips or chopped pecan nuts to the mixture instead of the dark chocolate chips, if you prefer. You can also add the finely grated rind of 1 orange for a chocolate and orange flavour.

A little bit fiddly to make but well worth the effort. Indulge in these tasty cakes with coffee, or serve them as a dessert with summer fruits.

Chocolate Rum Babas

1 Lightly oil 4 individual ring tins. In a large warmed mixing bowl, sift the flour and cocoa powder together. Stir in the yeast, salt, sugar and grated chocolate. In a separate bowl, beat the eggs together, add the milk and butter and beat until mixed.

2 Make a well in the centre of the dry ingredients and pour in the egg mixture, beating to mix to a batter. Beat for 10 minutes, ideally in an electric mixer with a dough hook. Divide the mixture between the tins – it should come halfway up the sides.

3 Place on a baking tray and cover with a damp tea towel. Leave in a warm place until the mixture rises almost to the tops of the tins. Bake in a preheated oven, 200°C/400°F/Gas Mark 6, for 15 minutes.

4 To make the syrup, gently heat all of the ingredients in a small pan. Turn out the babas and place on a rack placed above a tray to catch the syrup. Drizzle the syrup over the babas and leave for at least 2 hours for the syrup to soak in. Once or twice, spoon up the syrup that has dripped on to the tray and drizzle it over the babas again.

5 Fill the centre of the babas with whipped cream and sprinkle a little cocoa powder over the top. Serve the babas with fresh fruit, if desired.

SERVES 4

100 g/3½ oz strong plain flour
2 tbsp cocoa powder
6 g sachet easy-blend dried yeast
pinch of salt
1 tbsp caster sugar
40 g/1½ oz dark chocolate, grated
2 eggs
3 tbsp hand-hot milk
4 tbsp butter, melted

syrup
4 tbsp clear honey
2 tbsp water
4 tbsp rum

to serve
whipped cream
cocoa powder, to dust
fresh fruit (optional)

 challenging

3 hrs

15 mins

Children will enjoy making these as an introduction to chocolate cookery, and they keep well if stored in the refrigerator.

No-bake Chocolate Squares

MAKES 16

275 g/9½ oz dark chocolate
175 g/6 oz butter
4 tbsp golden syrup
2 tbsp dark rum (optional)
175 g/6 oz plain biscuits, such as Rich Tea
25 g/1 oz toasted rice cereal
50 g/1¾ oz chopped walnuts or pecan nuts
100 g/3½ oz glacé cherries, chopped roughly
25 g/1 oz white chocolate, to decorate

1 Place the dark chocolate in a large mixing bowl with the butter, syrup and rum, if using, and set over a saucepan of gently simmering water until melted, stirring until blended.

2 Break the biscuits into small pieces and stir into the chocolate mixture along with the rice cereal, nuts and cherries.

3 Line an 18-cm/7-inch square cake tin with baking paper. Pour the mixture into the tin and level the top, pressing down well with the back of a spoon. Chill for 2 hours.

4 To decorate, melt the white chocolate and drizzle it over the top of the cake in a random pattern. Leave to set. To serve, carefully turn out of the tin and remove the baking paper. Cut into 16 squares to serve.

⭐ very easy

🕐 2 hrs 15 mins

🕐 5 mins

🍽 COOK'S TIP

Brandy or an orange-flavoured liqueur can be used instead of the rum, if you prefer. Cherry brandy also works well.

Everyone loves chocolate brownies and these are so gooey and delicious they are impossible to resist!

Sticky Chocolate Brownies

1 Lightly grease a 20-cm/8-inch shallow square cake tin and line the base with baking paper.

2 Place the butter, sugars, dark chocolate and golden syrup in a heavy-based saucepan and heat gently, stirring until the mixture is well blended and smooth. Remove from the heat and leave to cool.

3 Beat together the eggs and chocolate or vanilla essence. Whisk in the cooled chocolate mixture.

4 Sift together the flour, cocoa powder and baking powder and fold carefully into the egg and chocolate mixture, using a metal spoon or spatula.

5 Spoon the mixture into the prepared tin and bake in a preheated oven, 180°C/350°F/Gas Mark 4, for 25 minutes, until the top is crisp and the edge of the cake is beginning to shrink away from the tin. The inside of the cake will still be quite stodgy and soft to the touch.

6 Leave the cake to cool completely in the tin, then cut it into squares to serve.

MAKES 9

100 g/3½ oz unsalted butter
175 g/6 oz caster sugar
75 g/2¾ oz dark muscovado sugar
125 g/4½ oz dark chocolate
1 tbsp golden syrup
2 eggs
1 tsp chocolate or vanilla essence
100 g/3½ oz plain flour
2 tbsp cocoa powder
½ tsp baking powder

🍮 **COOK'S TIP**

This cake can be well wrapped and frozen for up to 2 months. Defrost at room temperature for about 2 hours, or overnight in the refrigerator.

⭐⭐ easy
🕐 1 hr 20 mins
🕐 25 mins

Here, a traditional brownie mixture has a cream cheese ribbon through the centre and is topped with a delicious chocolate fudge icing.

Chocolate Fudge Brownies

MAKES 16

200 g/7 oz low-fat soft cheese
1/2 tsp vanilla essence
250 g/9 oz caster sugar
2 eggs
100 g/3 1/2 oz butter
3 tbsp cocoa powder
100 g/3 1/2 oz self-raising flour, sifted
50 g/1 3/4 oz pecan nuts, chopped, plus extra
    nuts to decorate (optional)

fudge icing
4 tbsp butter
1 tbsp milk
100 g/3 1/2 oz icing sugar
2 tbsp cocoa powder

1 Lightly grease a 20-cm/8-inch shallow square cake tin and line the base with baking paper.

2 Beat together the cheese, vanilla essence and 25 g/1 oz of the caster sugar until smooth, then set aside.

3 Beat the eggs and remaining caster sugar together until light and fluffy. Place the butter and cocoa powder in a small pan and heat gently, stirring until the butter melts and the mixture combines, then stir it into the egg mixture. Fold in the flour and nuts.

4 Pour half of the chocolate mixture into the tin and level the top. Carefully spread the soft cheese mixture over it, then cover it with the remaining brownie mixture. Bake in a preheated oven, 180°C/350°F/ Gas Mark 4, for 40–45 minutes. Cool in the tin.

5 To make the icing, melt the butter in the milk. Stir in the icing sugar and cocoa powder. Spread the icing over the brownies and decorate with pecan nuts, if using. Leave the icing to set, then cut into squares to serve.

🐾 COOK'S TIP

Omit the cheese layer if preferred. Use walnuts in place of the pecans.

easy

1 hr 20 mins

40–45 mins

Muffins are always popular and are so simple to make. You can make mini muffins as fabulous bite-sized treats for young children.

Chocolate Chip Muffins

1 Line 12 muffin tins with paper cases.

2 Place the margarine and sugar in a mixing bowl and beat with a wooden spoon until light and fluffy. Beat in the eggs, yogurt and milk until combined.

3 Sift the flour and bicarbonate of soda together and add to the mixture with the chocolate chips. Stir until just blended.

4 Spoon the mixture into the paper cases and bake in a preheated oven, 190°C/ 375°F/Gas Mark 5, for 25 minutes or until a fine skewer inserted into the centre comes out clean. Leave to cool in the tin for 5 minutes, then turn out on to a wire rack to cool completely.

MAKES 12

100 g/3½ oz soft margarine
225 g/8 oz caster sugar
2 large eggs
150 ml/5 fl oz full-fat natural yogurt
5 tbsp milk
275 g/9½ oz plain flour
1 tsp bicarbonate of soda
175 g/6 oz dark chocolate chips

 COOK'S TIP

The mixture can also be used to make 6 large or 24 mini muffins. Bake mini muffins for 10 minutes or until springy to the touch.

easy

45 mins

25 mins

A plain scone mixture is transformed into a chocoholic's treat by the simple addition of chocolate chips.

Chocolate Scones

MAKES 9

225 g/8 oz self-raising flour, sifted, plus flour
for dusting
5 tbsp butter
1 tbsp caster sugar
50 g/1¾ oz chocolate chips
about 150 ml/5 fl oz milk

1 Lightly grease a baking tray. Place the flour in a mixing bowl. Cut the butter into small pieces and rub it into the flour with your fingertips until the mixture resembles fine breadcrumbs.

2 Stir in the caster sugar and chocolate chips, then mix in enough milk to form a soft dough.

3 On a lightly floured surface, roll out the dough to form a rectangle measuring 10 x 15 cm/4 x 6 inches, about 2.5 cm/1 inch thick. Cut into 9 squares. Place the scones spaced well apart on the prepared baking tray.

4 Brush the scones with a little milk and bake in a preheated oven, 220°C/425°F/Gas Mark 7, for 10–12 minutes, until risen and golden.

easy

10 mins

10–12 mins

🍳 **COOK'S TIP**

To be at their best, scones should be served freshly baked and still warm. Split the warm scones and spread them with a little chocolate and hazelnut spread or a good dollop of whipped cream.

These croissants can be a bit fiddly to make, but the layers of flaky pastry enclosing a fabulous rich chocolate filling are worth the effort.

Pain *au* Chocolat

1 Lightly grease a baking tray. Sift the flour and salt into a mixing bowl and stir in the yeast. Rub in the fat with your fingertips. Add the egg and enough of the water to make a soft dough. Knead the dough for about 10 minutes, until smooth and elastic.

2 Roll the dough out to form a rectangle measuring 38 x 20 cm/15 x 8 inches. Divide the butter into 3 portions and dot one portion over two-thirds of the rectangle, leaving a small border around the edge.

3 Fold the rectangle into 3 by first folding the plain third of the dough over and then the other third. Seal the edges of the dough by pressing with a rolling pin. Give the dough a quarter turn so the sealed edges are at the top and bottom. Re-roll and fold (without adding butter), then wrap the dough and chill for 30 minutes.

4 Repeat Steps 2 and 3 twice, chilling the dough each time. Re-roll and fold twice more without butter. Chill for a final 30 minutes.

5 Roll the dough to a rectangle measuring 45 x 30 cm/18 x 12 inches, trim, and halve lengthways. Cut each half into 6 rectangles and brush with beaten egg. Place a chocolate square at one end of each rectangle and roll up to form a sausage. Press the ends together and place, seam-side down, on the baking tray. Cover and leave to rise for 40 minutes in a warm place. Brush with egg and bake in a preheated oven, 220°C/425°F/Gas Mark 7, for 20–25 minutes, until golden. Cool on a wire rack. Serve warm or cold.

MAKES 12

450 g/1 lb strong plain flour
½ tsp salt
6 g sachet easy-blend dried yeast
25 g/1 oz white vegetable fat
1 egg, beaten lightly
225 ml/8 fl oz hand-hot water
175 g/6 oz butter, softened
beaten egg, to seal and glaze
100 g/3½ oz dark chocolate, broken into 12 squares
icing sugar, to dust

✪✪✪✪ challenging

 4 hr 30 mins

20–25 mins

Pâtisserie cream is the traditional filling for éclairs, but if time is short you can fill them with whipped cream.

Chocolate Eclairs

MAKES 10

choux pastry
150 ml/5 fl oz water
5 tbsp butter, cut into small pieces
85 g/3 oz strong plain flour, sifted
2 eggs, beaten lightly

patisserie cream
2 eggs, beaten lightly
4 tbsp caster sugar
2 tbsp cornflour
300 ml/10 fl oz milk
¼ tsp vanilla essence

icing
2 tbsp butter
1 tbsp milk
1 tbsp cocoa powder
100 g/3½ oz icing sugar
a little white chocolate, melted

1 Lightly grease a baking tray. Place the water in a saucepan, add the butter and heat gently until the butter melts. Bring to a rolling boil, then remove the pan from the heat and add the flour in one go. Beat well until the mixture leaves the sides of the pan and forms a ball. Leave to cool slightly, then gradually beat in the eggs to form a smooth, glossy mixture. Spoon into a large piping bag fitted with a 1-cm/½-inch plain nozzle.

2 Sprinkle the baking tray with a little water. Pipe éclairs 7.5 cm/3 inches long, spaced well apart. Bake in a preheated oven, 200°C/400°F/Gas Mark 6, for 30–35 minutes or until crisp and golden. Make a small slit in each one to let the steam escape. Cool on a wire rack.

3 Meanwhile, make the pâtisserie cream. Whisk the eggs and sugar until thick and creamy, then whisk in the cornflour. Heat the milk until almost boiling and pour on to the eggs, whisking. Transfer to the pan and cook over a low heat, stirring until thick. Remove the pan from the heat and stir in the vanilla essence. Cover with baking paper and cool.

4 To make the icing, melt the butter with the milk in a pan, remove from the heat and stir in the cocoa and sugar. Split the éclairs lengthways and pipe in the pâtisserie cream. Spread the icing over the top of the éclairs. Spoon over the white chocolate, swirl in and leave to set.

★★★★ challenging
1 hr
30–35 mins

These melt-in-the-mouth meringues are ideal for a buffet dessert – pile them high in a pyramid for pure, bite-sized magic.

Chocolate Meringues

1 Line 2 baking trays with baking paper. Whisk the egg whites until standing in soft peaks, then gradually whisk in half of the sugar. Continue whisking until the mixture is very stiff and glossy.

2 Carefully fold in the remaining sugar, cornflour and grated chocolate with a metal spoon or spatula.

3 Spoon the mixture into a piping bag fitted with a large star or plain nozzle. Pipe 16 large rosettes or mounds on the lined baking trays.

4 Bake in a preheated oven, 140°C/275°F/Gas Mark 1, for about 1 hour, changing the position of the baking trays halfway through cooking. Without opening the oven door, turn off the oven and leave the meringues to cool in the oven. Once cold, carefully peel away the baking paper.

5 Melt the dark chocolate and spread it over the base of the meringues. Stand them upside down on a wire rack until the chocolate has set. Whip together the cream, icing sugar and brandy (if using), until the cream holds its shape. Spoon into a piping bag and pipe on to half of the meringues. Finish each with a second meringue and serve at once.

MAKES 8

4 egg whites
225 g/8 oz caster sugar
1 tsp cornflour
40 g/1½ oz dark chocolate, grated

to complete
100 g/3½ oz dark chocolate
150 ml/5 fl oz double cream
1 tbsp icing sugar
1 tbsp brandy (optional)

COOK'S TIP

To make mini meringues, use a star shaped nozzle and pipe about 24 small rosettes. Bake for about 40 minutes until crisp.

easy
1 hr 25 mins
1 hr

CHOCOLATE

These delicious chocolate and hazelnut biscuits are very simple to make, yet so effective. For very young children, leave out the chopped nuts.

Chocolate Hazelnut Palmiers

MAKES 26

375 g/13 oz ready-made puff pastry
8 tbsp chocolate hazelnut spread
50 g/1¾ oz chopped toasted hazelnuts
2 tbsp caster sugar

1 Lightly grease a baking tray. On a lightly floured surface, roll out the puff pastry to a rectangle measuring about 38 x 23 cm/15 x 9 inches.

2 Spread the chocolate hazelnut spread over the pastry using a palette knife, then scatter the chopped hazelnuts over the top.

3 Roll up one long side of the pastry to the centre, then roll up the other side so that they meet in the centre. Where the pieces meet, dampen the edges with a little water to join them. Using a sharp knife, cut into thin slices. Place each slice on to the prepared baking tray and flatten slightly with a palette knife. Sprinkle the slices with the caster sugar.

4 Bake in a preheated oven, 220°C/425°F/Gas Mark 7, for about 10–15 minutes, until golden. Transfer to a wire rack to cool.

(☺) **COOK'S TIP**

For an extra chocolate flavour, dip the cooked and cooled palmiers in melted dark chocolate to half-cover each biscuit.

⭐⭐ easy

5 mins

10–15 mins

These biscuits consist of a chewy coconut layer resting on a crisp chocolate biscuit base, cut into squares to serve.

Chocolate Coconut Squares

1 Grease a shallow 20-cm/8-inch square cake tin and line the base.

2 Crush the biscuits in a polythene bag with a rolling pin or process them in a food processor until fine. Melt the butter in a saucepan and stir in the crushed biscuits until well combined. Press the mixture into the base of the cake tin.

3 Beat together the evaporated milk, egg, vanilla and sugar until smooth. Stir in the flour and desiccated coconut. Pour the mixture over the biscuit base and level the top.

4 Bake in a preheated oven, 190°C/375°F/Gas Mark 5, for 30 minutes or until the coconut topping is firm and just golden.

5 Leave to cool in the cake tin for about 5 minutes, then cut into squares. Leave to cool completely in the tin.

6 Carefully remove the squares from the tin and place them on a board. Melt the dark chocolate (if using) and drizzle it over the squares to decorate them. Leave the chocolate to set before serving.

MAKES 9

225 g/8 oz dark chocolate digestive biscuits
6 tbsp butter or margarine
170 g/6 oz canned evaporated milk
1 egg, beaten
1 tsp vanilla essence
2 tbsp caster sugar
6 tbsp self-raising flour, sifted
125 g/4½ oz desiccated coconut
50 g/1¾ oz dark chocolate (optional)

COOK'S TIP

Store the squares in an airtight tin for up to 4 days. They can be frozen, undecorated, for up to 2 months. Defrost at room temperature.

moderate
1 hr 15 mins
30 mins

A favourite with children, this version of crispy cakes has been given a new twist which is sure to be popular.

Chocolate Crispy Bites

MAKES 16

white layer
4 tbsp butter
1 tbsp golden syrup
150 g/5½ oz white chocolate, broken into pieces
50 g/1¾ oz toasted rice cereal

dark layer
4 tbsp butter
2 tbsp golden syrup
125 g/4½ oz dark chocolate, broken into pieces
75 g/2¾ oz toasted rice cereal

1 Grease a 20-cm/8-inch square cake tin and line with baking paper.

2 To make the white chocolate layer, melt the butter, golden syrup and white chocolate in a bowl set over a saucepan of gently simmering water. Remove from the heat and stir in the rice cereal until it is well combined. Press into the prepared tin and level the surface.

3 To make the dark chocolate layer, melt the butter, golden syrup and dark chocolate in a bowl set over a pan of gently simmering water. Remove from the heat and stir in the rice cereal. Pour the dark chocolate layer over the hardened white chocolate layer and chill until hardened.

4 Turn out of the cake tin and cut into small squares, using a sharp knife.

easy
45 mins
5–10 mins

These unusual biscuit treats are delicious served with coffee. They also make an ideal dessert biscuit to serve with ice cream.

Dutch Macaroons

1 Cover 2 baking trays with rice paper. Whisk the egg whites in a large mixing bowl until stiff, then fold in the sugar and ground almonds.

2 Place the mixture in a large piping bag fitted with a 1-cm/½-inch plain nozzle and pipe fingers, about 7.5 cm/ 3 inches long, allowing space for the mixture to spread during cooking.

3 Bake in a preheated oven, 180°C/350°F/Gas Mark 4, for 15–20 minutes, until golden. Transfer to a wire rack and leave to cool. Remove the excess rice paper from around the edges.

4 Melt the chocolate and dip the base of each biscuit into the chocolate. Place the macaroons on a sheet of baking paper and leave to set.

5 Pipe any remaining chocolate over the top of the biscuits (you may have to reheat the chocolate in order to do this). Leave to set before serving.

MAKES 20

rice paper
2 egg whites
225 g/8 oz caster sugar
175 g/6 oz ground almonds
225 g/8 oz dark chocolate

🍳 COOK'S TIP

Rice paper is edible so you can just break off the excess from around the edge of the biscuits. Remove it completely before dipping the macaroons in the chocolate, if you prefer.

easy

40 mins

15–20 mins

Wonderfully rich, it is difficult to say 'No' to these biscuits, which consist of a crunchy base, a creamy caramel layer and a chocolate top.

Chocolate Caramel Squares

MAKES 16

100 g/3½ oz soft margarine
4 tbsp light muscovado sugar
125 g/4½ oz plain flour, sifted
40 g/1½ oz rolled oats

caramel filling
2 tbsp butter
2 tbsp light muscovado sugar
200 g/7 oz canned condensed milk

topping
100 g/3½ oz dark chocolate
25 g/1 oz white chocolate (optional)

1 Beat together the margarine and muscovado sugar in a bowl until light and fluffy. Beat in the flour and the rolled oats. Use your fingertips to bring the mixture together, if necessary.

2 Press the mixture into the base of a shallow 20-cm/8-inch square cake tin.

3 Bake in a preheated oven, 180°C/350°F/Gas Mark 4, for 25 minutes or until just golden and firm. Cool in the tin.

4 Place the ingredients for the caramel filling in a pan and heat gently, stirring, until the sugar has dissolved and the ingredients combine. Gradually bring to the boil over a very low heat, then boil very gently for 3–4 minutes, stirring constantly until thickened.

5 Pour the caramel filling over the biscuit base in the tin and leave to set.

6 Melt the dark chocolate and spread it over the caramel. If using the white chocolate, melt it and pipe lines of white chocolate over the dark chocolate. Using a cocktail stick or a skewer, feather the white chocolate into the dark chocolate. Leave to set. Cut into squares to serve.

★★★ moderate

🕐 40 mins

🕐 25 mins

🍳 **COOK'S TIP**

If liked, you can line the tin with baking paper so that the biscuit can be lifted out before cutting into pieces.

Turn ordinary flapjacks into something special with the addition of chocolate chips. Use white rather than dark chocolate chips, if you prefer.

Chocolate Chip Flapjacks

1 Lightly grease a shallow 20-cm/8-inch square cake tin.

2 Place the butter, caster sugar and golden syrup in a saucepan and cook over a low heat, stirring, until the butter and sugar melt and the mixture is thoroughly combined.

3 Remove the pan from the heat and stir in the rolled oats until they are well coated. Add the chocolate chips and the sultanas and mix well to combine. Turn into the prepared tin and press down well.

4 Bake in a preheated oven, 180°C/350°F/Gas Mark 4, for 30 minutes. Cool slightly, then mark into fingers. When almost cold, cut into bars or squares and transfer to a wire rack to cool completely.

MAKES 12

125 g/4½ oz butter
75 g/2¾ oz caster sugar
1 tbsp golden syrup
350 g/12 oz rolled oats
75 g/2¾ oz dark chocolate chips
50 g/1¾ oz sultanas

 COOK'S TIP

The flapjacks will keep in an airtight container for up to 1 week, but they are so delicious they are unlikely to last that long!

★★ easy
40 mins
30 mins

No chocolate cook's repertoire would be complete without a chocolate chip cookie recipe. This recipe can be used to make several variations.

Chocolate Chip Cookies

MAKES 18

175 g/6 oz plain flour
1 tsp baking powder
125 g/4½ oz soft margarine
85 g/3 oz light muscovado sugar
5 tbsp caster sugar
½ tsp vanilla essence
1 egg
125 g/4½ oz dark chocolate chips

1 Sift the flour and baking powder into a large mixing bowl, add the margarine, sugars, vanilla essence, egg and chocolate chips and beat until thoroughly combined.

2 Lightly grease 2 baking trays. Place tablespoonfuls of the mixture on the baking trays, spacing them well apart to allow for spreading during cooking.

3 Bake in a preheated oven, 190°C/375°F/Gas Mark 5, for 10–12 minutes or until the cookies are golden brown.

4 Using a palette knife, transfer the cookies to a wire rack and let them cool completely before serving.

⭐ very easy
🕐 35 mins
🕐 10 mins

🍳 **COOK'S TIP**

For Chocolate and Nut Cookies, add 40 g/1½ oz chopped hazelnuts to the basic mixture. For White Chocolate Chip Cookies, use white chocolate chips instead of the dark chocolate chips.

This buttery chocolate shortbread is the perfect addition to the biscuit tin of any chocoholic.

Chocolate Shortbread

1 Place all of the ingredients in a large mixing bowl and beat together until they form a dough. Knead the dough lightly.

2 Lightly grease a baking tray. Place the dough on the baking tray and roll or press out to form a 20-cm/8-inch circle.

3 Pinch the edges of the dough with your fingertips to form a decorative edge. Prick the dough all over with a fork and then mark it into 12 wedges, using a sharp knife.

4 Bake in a preheated oven, 160°C/325°F/Gas Mark 3, for 40 minutes, until firm and golden. Leave to cool slightly before cutting into wedges. Transfer to a wire rack to cool completely.

MAKES 12

175 g/6 oz plain flour, sifted
1 tbsp cocoa powder
4 tbsp caster sugar
150 g/5½ oz butter, softened
50 g/1¾ oz dark chocolate, chopped finely

COOK'S TIP

For round shortbread cookies, roll out the dough on a lightly floured surface to 8 mm/⅜ inch thick. Cut out 7.5-cm/3-inch rounds with a biscuit cutter. Transfer to a greased baking tray and bake as above.

very easy

40 mins

40 mins

CHOCOLATE

These biscuits have a fabulously light, melting texture. You can leave them plain, but for real indulgence, dip them in melted chocolate.

Viennese Chocolate Fingers

MAKES 18

125 g/4½ oz unsalted butter
6 tbsp icing sugar
175 g/6 oz self-raising flour, sifted
3 tbsp cornflour
200 g/7 oz dark chocolate

1 Lightly grease 2 baking trays. Beat the butter and sugar in a mixing bowl until light and fluffy. Gradually beat in the flour and cornflour.

2 Melt 75 g/2¾ oz of the dark chocolate and beat into the biscuit dough.

3 Place the mixture in a piping bag fitted with a large star nozzle and pipe fingers about 5 cm/2 inches long on the baking trays, slightly spaced apart to allow for spreading.

4 Bake in a preheated oven, 190°C/375°F/Gas Mark 5, for 12–15 minutes. Leave to cool slightly on the baking trays, then transfer with a spatula to a wire rack and leave to cool completely.

5 Melt the remaining chocolate and dip one end of each biscuit in the chocolate, allowing the excess to drip back into the bowl. Place the biscuits on a sheet of baking paper and leave to set before serving.

⊛ COOK'S TIP

If the biscuit dough is too thick to pipe, beat in a little milk to thin it out a little.

✪✪✪   moderate

🕐   1 hr

🕐   15 mins

If you thought of pretzels as savouries, then think again. These are fun to make and prove that pretzels come in a sweet variety, too.

Chocolate Pretzels

1 Lightly grease a baking tray. Beat together the butter and sugar in a mixing bowl until light and fluffy. Beat in the egg.

2 Sift together the flour and cocoa powder and gradually beat in to form a soft dough. Use your fingers to incorporate the last of the flour and bring the dough together. Chill for 15 minutes.

3 Break small pieces from the dough and roll into thin sausage shapes about 10 cm/4 inches long and 5 mm/¼ inch thick. Twist into pretzel shapes by making a circle, then twisting the ends through each other. Place the pretzels on the prepared baking tray, slightly spaced apart to allow for spreading during cooking.

4 Bake in a preheated oven, 190°C/375°F/Gas Mark 5, for 8–12 minutes. Leave the pretzels to cool slightly on the baking tray, then transfer to a wire rack to cool completely.

5 Melt the butter and chocolate in a bowl set over a pan of gently simmering water, stirring to combine. Dip half of each pretzel into the chocolate and allow the excess chocolate to drip back into the bowl. Place the pretzels on a sheet of baking paper and leave to set.

6 When set, dust the plain side of each pretzel with icing sugar.

MAKES 30
100 g/3½ oz unsalted butter
100 g/3½ oz caster sugar
1 egg
225 g/8 oz plain flour
2 tbsp cocoa powder

to finish
1 tbsp butter
100 g/3½ oz dark chocolate
icing sugar, to dust

★★★★ challenging
1 hr 30 mins
8–12 mins

A good everyday biscuit, these wheatmeals will keep well in an airtight container for at least a week. Dip in white, milk or dark chocolate.

Chocolate Wheatmeals

MAKES 20

6 tbsp butter
100 g/3½ oz demerara sugar
1 egg
25 g/1 oz wheatgerm
125 g/4½ oz wholemeal self-raising flour, sifted
6 tbsp self-raising flour, sifted
125 g/4½ oz dark, milk or white chocolate

1 Lightly grease a baking tray. Beat the butter and sugar until fluffy. Add the egg and beat well. Stir in the wheatgerm and flours. Bring the mixture together with your hands.

2 Roll rounded teaspoons of the mixture into balls and place on the prepared baking tray, allowing room for the biscuits to spread during cooking.

3 Flatten the biscuits slightly with the prongs of a fork. Bake in a preheated oven, 180°C/350°F/Gas Mark 4, for 15–20 minutes, until golden. Leave to cool on the baking tray for a few minutes before transferring to a wire rack to cool completely.

4 Melt the chocolate, then dip each biscuit in the chocolate to cover the base and come a little way up the sides. Allow the excess chocolate to drip back into the bowl.

5 Place the biscuits on a sheet of baking paper and leave to set in a cool place before serving.

⭐⭐   easy
🕐   1 hr
🕐   15–20 mins

👨‍🍳 **COOK'S TIP**

These biscuits can be frozen very successfully. Freeze them at the end of Step 3 for up to 3 months. Defrost and then dip them in melted chocolate.

No Sicilian celebration is complete without cannoli. If you can't find the moulds, use large dried pasta tubes, covered with foil, shiny side out.

Cannoli

1 Combine the lemon juice, water and egg. Put the flour, sugar, spice and salt in a food processor and quickly process. Add the butter, then, with the motor running, pour the egg mixture through the feeder tube. Process until the mixture just forms a dough.

2 Turn the dough out on to a lightly floured surface and knead lightly. Wrap and chill for at least 1 hour.

3 Meanwhile, make the filling. Beat the ricotta cheese until smooth. Sift in the icing sugar, then beat in the remaining ingredients. Cover and chill until required.

4 Roll out the dough on a floured surface until 2 mm/¹⁄₁₆ inch thick. Using a ruler, cut out 8.5 x 7.5-cm/3 ¹⁄₂ x 3-inch pieces, re-rolling and cutting the trimmings, making about 20 pieces in all.

5 Heat 5 cm/2 inches of oil in a saucepan to 190°C/375°F. Roll a piece of pastry around a greased cannoli mould, to just overlap the edge. Seal with egg white, pressing firmly. Repeat with all the moulds you have. Fry 2 or 3 moulds until the cannoli are golden, crisp and bubbly.

6 Remove with a slotted spoon and drain on paper towels. Leave until cool, then carefully slide off the moulds. Repeat with the remaining cannoli.

7 Store unfilled in an airtight container for up to 2 days. Pipe in the filling no more than 30 minutes before serving to prevent the pastry from becoming soggy. Sift icing sugar over and serve.

MAKES 20

3 tbsp lemon juice
3 tbsp water
1 large egg
250 g/9 oz plain flour, sifted, plus extra for dusting
1 tbsp caster sugar
1 tsp ground mixed spice
pinch of salt
2 tbsp butter, softened
sunflower oil, for deep-frying
1 small egg white, beaten lightly
icing sugar

filling
750 g/1 lb 10 oz ricotta cheese, drained
4 tbsp icing sugar
1 tsp vanilla essence
finely grated rind of 1 large orange
4 tbsp very finely chopped glacé fruit
50 g/1³⁄₄ oz dark chocolate, grated
pinch of ground cinnamon
2 tbsp Marsala or orange juice

 challenging
1 hr 45 mins
15–20 mins

Pine kernels and orange rind are popular ingredients in Mediterranean dishes – here they add a twist of flavour to luscious chocolate tartlets.

Pine Kernel Tartlets

SERVES 8

60 g/2 oz continental chocolate with at
    least 70% cocoa solids, broken into pieces
5 tbsp unsalted butter
175 g/6 oz plus 2 tbsp caster sugar
6 tbsp light brown sugar
6 tbsp milk
3½ tbsp golden syrup
finely grated rind of 2 large oranges
2 tbsp freshly squeezed orange juice
1 tsp vanilla essence
3 large eggs, beaten lightly
100 g/3½ oz pine kernels

pastry
250 g/9 oz plain flour
pinch of salt
100 g/3½ oz butter
115 g/4 oz icing sugar
1 large egg
2 large egg yolks

moderate

1 hr 40 mins

45 mins

1 To make the pastry, sift the flour and a pinch of salt into a bowl. Make a well in the centre and add the butter, icing sugar, whole egg and egg yolks. Using your fingertips, mix the ingredients in the well into a paste.

2 Gradually incorporate the flour to make a soft dough. Quickly and lightly knead the dough. Shape into a ball, wrap in clingfilm and chill for at least 1 hour.

3 Roll the pastry into 8 circles, each 15 cm/6 inch across. Use to line 8 loose-bottomed 10-cm/4-inch tartlet tins. Line each with baking paper and fill with baking beans. Chill for 10 minutes.

4 Bake in a preheated oven, 200°C/400°F/Gas Mark 6, for 5 minutes. Remove the paper and beans and bake for a further 8 minutes. Leave to cool on a wire rack. Reduce the oven temperature to 180°C/350°F/Gas Mark 4.

5 Meanwhile, put the chocolate and butter in a saucepan and stir over a medium heat until blended.

6 Stir in the remaining ingredients. Spoon the filling into the tartlet cases on a baking tray. Bake for 25–30 minutes or until the tops puff up and crack and feel set. Cover with baking paper for the final 5 minutes if the pastry is browning too much. Transfer to a wire rack and leave to cool for at least 15 minutes before unmoulding. Serve warm or at room temperature.

These chunky cookies simply melt in the mouth and the white chocolate gives them a deliciously rich flavour.

White Chocolate Cookies

1 Lightly grease 4 baking trays. In a large mixing bowl, cream together the butter and sugar until light and fluffy. Gradually add the beaten egg, beating well after each addition.

2 Sift the flour and salt into the creamed mixture and blend well. Stir in the white chocolate chunks and the chopped Brazil nuts.

3 Place heaped teaspoons of the white chocolate mixture on the prepared baking trays. Do not put more than 6 teaspoons of the mixture on to each baking tray as the cookies will spread considerably during cooking.

4 Bake in a preheated oven, 190°C/375°F/Gas Mark 5, for 10–12 minutes or until just golden brown.

5 Transfer the cookies to wire racks and leave until completely cold before serving.

MAKES 24

125 g/4½ oz butter, softened
125 g/4½ oz soft brown sugar
1 egg, beaten
200 g/7 oz self-raising flour
pinch of salt
125 g/4½ oz white chocolate, chopped roughly
50 g/1¾ oz Brazil nuts, chopped

COOK'S TIP

Use plain or milk chocolate instead of white chocolate, if you prefer.

⭐⭐ easy
🕐 40 mins
🕐 10–12 mins

Classic gooey macaroons are always a favourite for teatime: they are made even better by the addition of rich dark chocolate.

Chocolate Macaroons

MAKES 18

2 egg whites
pinch of salt
200 g/7 oz caster sugar
125 g/4½ oz ground almonds
75 g/2¾ oz dark chocolate, melted and cooled
desiccated coconut, for sprinkling (optional)

1 Grease 2 baking trays and line with baking paper or rice paper.

2 In a mixing bowl, whisk the egg whites with the salt until they form soft peaks. Gradually whisk in the caster sugar, then fold in the almonds and cooled melted chocolate.

3 Place heaped teaspoonfuls of the mixture spaced well apart on the prepared baking trays and spread into circles about 6 cm/2½ inches across. Sprinkle with desiccated coconut, if using.

4 Bake in a preheated oven, 150°C/300°F/Gas Mark 2, for about 25 minutes or until firm.

5 Leave to cool before carefully lifting from the baking trays. Transfer to a wire rack and leave to cool completely before serving.

⚉ **COOK'S TIP**

For a traditional finish, top each chocolate macaroon with half a glacé cherry before baking.

★★★ moderate
🕐 1 hr
🕐 25 mins

These luxury biscuits will be popular at any time of the year, but make a particularly wonderful treat at Christmas.

Florentines

1 Line two large baking trays with baking paper.

2 Heat the butter and caster sugar in a small saucepan until the butter has just melted and the sugar dissolved. Remove the pan from the heat.

3 Stir in the flour and mix well. Stir in the chopped almonds, mixed peel, raisins, cherries and lemon rind. Place teaspoonfuls of the mixture well apart on the baking trays.

4 Bake in a preheated oven, 180°C/350°F/Gas Mark 4, for 10 minutes or until lightly golden.

5 As soon as the florentines are removed from the oven, press the edges into neat shapes while still on the baking trays, using a biscuit cutter. Leave to cool on the baking trays until firm, then carefully transfer to a wire rack to cool completely.

6 Spread the melted chocolate over the smooth side of each florentine. As the chocolate begins to set, mark wavy lines in it with a fork. Leave the florentines until set, chocolate side up.

MAKES 10

4 tbsp butter
4 tbsp caster sugar
3 tbsp plain flour, sifted
50 g/1³/₄ oz almonds, chopped
50 g/1³/₄ oz chopped mixed peel
25 g/1 oz raisins, chopped
25 g/1 oz glacé cherries, chopped
finely grated rind of ¹/₂ lemon
125 g/4¹/₂ oz dark chocolate, melted

🍪 **COOK'S TIP**

Replace the dark chocolate with white chocolate or, for a dramatic effect, cover half of the florentines in dark chocolate and half in white.

  moderate

50 mins

10 mins

These little cakes look wonderful, and are well worth the preparation time. The magical combination of flavours is out of this world.

Chestnut Cream Squares

MAKES 30

base layer
6 tbsp unsalted butter
4 tbsp icing sugar
85 g/3 oz dark chocolate, melted
4 eggs, separated
100 g/3½ oz caster sugar
90 g/3¼ oz plain flour, sifted
5 tbsp Morello cherry jam
3 tbsp kirsch

dark layer
100 ml/3½ fl oz milk
4 tsp caster sugar
¼ tsp vanilla essence
1 egg yolk
1 tbsp cornflour
generous 2 tbsp icing sugar
100 g/3½ oz dark chocolate, melted
300 ml/10 fl oz double cream, whipped

white layer
500 ml/18 fl oz double cream
1 tbsp icing sugar

chestnut layer
435 g/15¼ oz canned chestnut purée
4 tsp dark rum
2 tsp caster sugar
30 cherries, to decorate

⭐⭐⭐⭐ challenging
🕐 12 hrs 45 mins
🕐 55–60 mins

1 Line a 30 x 25 x 5-cm/12 x 10 x 2-inch rectangular cake tin. For the base layer, mix the butter, icing sugar and chocolate. Beat in the egg yolks, 1 at a time.

2 Whisk the egg whites until soft peaks form, then whisk in the caster sugar until stiff and glossy. Fold in the chocolate mixture and the flour. Spoon into the tin and smooth the surface. Bake in a preheated oven, 180°C/350°F/Gas Mark 4, for 30 minutes. Leave to cool.

3 Bring the jam to the boil in a small pan, strain and cool. Turn out the base layer. Wash and dry the tin and line with baking paper. Return the base layer to the tin. Sprinkle with the kirsch and spread with the jam.

4 For the dark layer, put the milk, caster sugar and vanilla in a pan and bring to the boil. Mix the egg yolk, cornflour and 2 tablespoons of the hot milk in a bowl, then add back to the pan of milk. Cook, stirring, for 3–5 minutes, until thickened. Stir in the icing sugar and chocolate. Remove from the heat and stir in the cream. Spread in the tin, cover and freeze for 1½–2 hours.

5 Make the white layer: whisk the cream with the sugar until thick, then spread over the dark layer. Cover and freeze for 8 hours.

6 Remove the cake from the tin. Beat together the chestnut purée, rum and sugar. Cut the cake into 30 squares, pipe each with a swirl of chestnut mixture and top with a cherry. Chill for 30 minutes before serving.

These crisp Italian biscotti are made with polenta – fine cornmeal – as well as flour, to give them an interesting texture.

Chocolate Pistachio Biscotti

1 Lightly grease a baking tray. Put the butter and chocolate in the top of a double boiler or in a heatproof bowl set over a pan of barely simmering water. Stir over a low heat until melted and smooth. Remove from the heat and cool slightly.

2 Sift the flour and baking powder into a bowl and mix in the caster sugar, polenta, lemon rind, liqueur, egg and pistachios. Stir in the chocolate mixture and mix to a soft dough.

3 Dust your hands with flour, divide the dough in half and shape each piece into a 28-cm/11-inch cylinder. Transfer the dough cylinders to the prepared baking tray and flatten, with the palm of your hand, to about 2 cm/³⁄₄ inch thick. Bake in a preheated oven, 160°C/325°F/Gas Mark 3, for about 20 minutes, until firm to the touch.

4 Remove the baking tray from the oven and allow the cooked pieces to cool. When cool, put the cooked pieces on to a chopping board and slice them diagonally into thin biscuits. Return them to the baking tray and bake for a further 10 minutes, until crisp. Remove from the oven, and transfer to a wire rack to cool. Dust lightly with icing sugar.

MAKES 24

2 tbsp unsalted butter
175 g/6 oz dark chocolate, broken into pieces
300 g/10½ oz self-raising flour
1½ tsp baking powder
85 g/3 oz caster sugar
55 g/2 oz polenta
finely grated rind of 1 lemon
2 tsp amaretto liqueur
1 egg, beaten lightly
85 g/3 oz shelled pistachio nuts, roughly chopped
2 tbsp icing sugar, to dust

COOK'S TIP

Amaretto liqueur is flavoured with apricot kernels and has a flavour strongly reminiscent of almonds. If you prefer, use an orange liqueur.

★★★ moderate
55 mins
35 mins

Sweets *and* Drinks

There is nothing quite so nice as home-made chocolates
and sweets – they leave the average box of chocolates in
the shade! You'll find recipes in this chapter to suit
everybody's taste. Wonderful, rich, melt-in-the-mouth
Rum Truffles, Marzipan Cherries, Rocky Road Bites and rich
Chocolate Liqueurs – they're all here. There is even some
Easy Chocolate Fudge, so there is no need to fiddle about
with sugar thermometers.

Looking for something to wash it all down? We have
included delightfully cool summer chocolate drinks and,
for warmth and comfort on winter nights, hot drinks that
will simply put instant hot chocolate to shame. Enjoy!

Young children will love these chewy bites. You can vary the ingredients and use different nuts and dried fruit according to taste.

Rocky Road Bites

MAKES **18**

125 g/4½ oz milk chocolate
55 g/2 oz mini multi-
 coloured marshmallows
25 g/1 oz chopped walnuts
25 g/1 oz ready-to-eat dried
 apricots, chopped

1 Line a baking tray with baking paper and set aside.

2 Break the milk chocolate into small pieces and place in a large mixing bowl. Set the bowl over a pan of simmering water and stir until the chocolate has melted.

3 Stir in the marshmallows, walnuts and apricots and toss in the melted chocolate until well covered.

4 Place heaped teaspoons of the mixture on to the prepared baking tray. Chill in the refrigerator until set.

5 Once set, remove the sweets from the baking paper. They can be placed in paper sweet cases to serve, if desired.

⊛ **COOK'S TIP**

If you cannot find mini marshmallows, use large ones and snip them into smaller pieces with kitchen scissors before mixing them into the melted chocolate in Step 3.

⊛ very easy
◔ 40 mins
◷ 5 mins

This is the easiest fudge to make – for a really rich flavour, use a good dark chocolate with a high cocoa content, ideally at least 70 per cent.

Easy Chocolate Fudge

1 Lightly grease a 20-cm/8-inch square cake tin.

2 Break the chocolate into pieces and place in a large saucepan with the butter and condensed milk.

3 Heat gently, stirring, until the chocolate and butter melt and the mixture is smooth. Do not allow to boil.

4 Remove from the heat. Beat in the vanilla essence, then beat the mixture for a few minutes until thickened. Pour it into the prepared tin and level the top.

5 Chill the mixture in the refrigerator until firm.

6 Tip the fudge out on to a chopping board and cut into squares to serve.

MAKES 25

500 g/1 lb 2 oz dark chocolate
75 g/2¾ oz unsalted butter
400 g/14 oz canned condensed milk
¼ tsp vanilla essence

 COOK'S TIP

Store the fudge in an airtight container in a cool, dry place for up to 1 month. Do not freeze.

⭐⭐ easy

🕐 1 hr 10 mins

🕐 5 mins

Chocolate, nuts and dried fruit – the perfect combination – are all found in this simple-to-make fudge.

Fruit *and* Nut Fudge

MAKES 25

250 g/9 oz dark chocolate
2 tbsp butter
4 tbsp evaporated milk
450 g/1 lb icing sugar, sifted
50 g/1¾ oz hazelnuts, chopped roughly
50 g/1¾ oz sultanas

1 Lightly grease a 20-cm/8-inch square cake tin.

2 Break the chocolate into pieces and place it in a heatproof bowl with the butter and evaporated milk. Set the bowl over a pan of gently simmering water and stir until the chocolate and butter have melted and the ingredients are well combined.

3 Remove the bowl from the heat and gradually beat in the icing sugar. Stir the hazelnuts and sultanas into the mixture. Press the fudge into the prepared tin and level the top. Chill until firm.

4 Tip the fudge out on to a chopping board and cut into squares. Place in paper sweet cases. Chill until required.

easy
1 hr 10 mins
5 mins

🍳 COOK'S TIP

Vary the nuts used in this recipe; try making the fudge with almonds, Brazil nuts, walnuts or pecans.

These tasty cherry and marzipan sweets are easy to make. Serve as petits fours at the end of a meal or as an indulgent nibble at any time of day.

Marzipan Cherries

1 Line a baking tray with a sheet of baking paper.

2 Cut the cherries in half and place them in a small bowl. Add the rum or brandy and stir well to coat. Leave the cherries to soak for at least 1 hour, stirring occasionally.

3 Divide the marzipan into 24 pieces and roll each piece into a ball. Press half a cherry into the top of each marzipan ball.

4 Break the chocolate into pieces, place in a bowl and set over a pan of hot water. Stir until all the chocolate has melted.

5 Dip each sweet into the melted chocolate using a cocktail stick, allowing the excess to drip back into the bowl. Place the coated cherries on the baking paper and chill until set.

6 If liked, melt a little extra chocolate and drizzle it over the top of the coated cherries. Leave to set.

MAKES 25

12 glacé cherries
2 tbsp rum or brandy
250 g/9 oz marzipan
125 g/5½ oz dark chocolate
extra milk, dark or white chocolate, to decorate (optional)

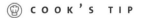 **COOK'S TIP**

As an alternative, flatten the marzipan and use it to mould around the cherries to cover them, then dip in the chocolate as above.

 ✪✪✪ moderate

🕐 1 hr 30 mins

🕐 5 mins

These tasty chocolate cups are filled with a delicious liqueur-flavoured filling. Use your favourite liqueur to flavour the cream.

Chocolate Liqueurs

MAKES 40

100 g/3½ oz dark chocolate, melted
about 5 glacé cherries, halved
about 10 hazelnuts or macadamia nuts
150 ml/5 fl oz double cream
2 tbsp icing sugar
4 tbsp liqueur

to finish
50 g/1¾ oz dark chocolate, melted
a little white chocolate, melted
white chocolate Quick Curls (see page 15)
extra nuts and cherries

1 Line a baking tray with a sheet of baking paper. Spoon the chocolate into 20 paper sweet cases, spreading up the sides with a small spoon or pastry brush. Place upside down on the prepared baking tray and leave to set.

2 Carefully peel away the paper cases. Place a cherry half or a nut in the base of each chocolate cup.

3 To make the filling, place the double cream in a bowl and sift the icing sugar on top. Whisk the cream until it is just holding its shape, then whisk in the liqueur.

4 Place the cream in a piping bag fitted with a 1-cm/½-inch plain nozzle and pipe a little into each chocolate case. Chill for 20 minutes.

5 To finish, spoon the melted dark chocolate over the cream to cover it and pipe the melted white chocolate on top, swirling it into the dark chocolate with a cocktail stick. Leave to harden. Alternatively, cover the cream with the melted dark chocolate and decorate with white chocolate curls before setting. Or place a small piece of nut or cherry on top of the cream and then cover with dark chocolate.

COOK'S TIP

Sweet cases can vary in size. Use the smallest you can find for this recipe.

challenging

1 hr

5 mins

A creamy, orange-flavoured chocolate filling in white chocolate cups makes a wonderful treat.

Collettes

1 Line a baking tray with a sheet of baking paper. Spoon the melted white chocolate into 20 paper sweet cases, spreading it up the sides with a small pastry brush. Place upside down on the prepared baking tray and leave to set.

2 When set, carefully peel away the paper cases.

3 To make the filling, put the melted orange-flavoured chocolate in a mixing bowl with the double cream and the icing sugar. Beat until smooth. Chill until the mixture becomes firm enough to pipe, stirring occasionally.

4 Place the filling in a piping bag fitted with a star nozzle and pipe a little into each case. Chill until they are required.

MAKES 20

100 g/3½ oz white chocolate, melted

filling
150 g/5½ oz orange-flavoured dark chocolate, melted
150 ml/5 fl oz double cream
2 tbsp icing sugar

 COOK'S TIP

If the paper sweet cases do not hold their shape well, use 2 cases to make a double thickness mould. Foil cases are firmer, so use these if you can find them.

⭐⭐⭐ moderate

🕐 40 mins

🕐 5 mins

Small pastry cases are filled with a rich chocolate filling to serve as petits fours. Use small individual tartlet tins to make the pastry cases.

Mini Chocolate Tartlets

MAKES 18

175 g/6 oz plain flour, plus flour for dusting
6 tbsp butter
1 tbsp caster sugar
about 1 tbsp water

filling
100 g/3½ oz full-fat soft cheese
2 tbsp caster sugar
1 small egg, beaten lightly
50 g/1¾ oz dark chocolate, melted

to decorate
150 ml/5 fl oz double cream
dark chocolate Quick Curls (see page 15)
cocoa powder, to dust

1 Sift the flour into a mixing bowl. Cut the butter into small pieces and rub in with your fingertips until the mixture resembles fine breadcrumbs. Stir in the sugar. Add enough water to mix to a soft dough, then cover and chill for 15 minutes.

2 Roll out the pastry on a lightly floured surface and use to line 18 mini tartlet tins or mini muffin tins. Prick the bases with a cocktail stick.

3 Beat together the full-fat soft cheese and the sugar. Beat in the egg and the melted chocolate. Spoon into the pastry cases and bake in a preheated oven, 190°C/375°F/Gas Mark 5, for 15 minutes, until the pastry is crisp and the filling set. Place the tins on a wire rack to cool completely.

4 Chill the tartlets. Whip the cream until it is just holding its shape. Place in a piping bag fitted with a star nozzle. Pipe rosettes of cream on top of the tartlets. Decorate with Quick Curls and dust with cocoa powder.

⭐⭐⭐ moderate
🕐 1 hr 30 mins
🕐 15 mins

COOK'S TIP

The tartlets can be made up to 3 days ahead. Decorate on the day of serving, preferably no more than 4 hours in advance.

These unusual cone-shaped mint-cream chocolates make a change from the more usual cup shape, and are perfect as an after-dinner chocolate.

Mini Chocolate Cones

1 Cut 10 x 7.5-cm/3-inch circles of baking paper. Cut a straight line from the edge to the centre of each circle, then shape into a cone and secure on the outside with sticky tape.

2 Using a small pastry brush or clean artists' brush, brush the inside of each cone with the melted chocolate.

3 Brush a second layer of chocolate on the inside of the cones and leave to chill until set. Carefully peel away the paper.

4 Place the double cream, icing sugar and crème de menthe in a mixing bowl and whip until just holding its shape. Place in a piping bag fitted with a star nozzle and pipe the mixture into the chocolate cones.

5 Decorate the cones with chocolate coffee beans (if using) and chill in the refrigerator until required.

MAKES 10

75 g/2¾ oz dark chocolate, melted
100 ml/3½ fl oz double cream
1 tbsp icing sugar
1 tbsp crème de menthe
chocolate coffee beans, to decorate (optional)

🍴 **COOK'S TIP**

The chocolate cones can be made in advance and kept in the refrigerator for up to 1 week. Do not fill them more than 2 hours before you are going to serve them.

✪✪✪✪ challenging
🕐 40 mins
🕐 5 mins

Truffles are always popular. They make a fabulous gift or, served with coffee, are a perfect end to a meal.

Rum Truffles

MAKES 20

125 g/4½ oz dark chocolate
small knob of butter
2 tbsp rum
50 g/1¾ oz desiccated coconut
100 g/3½ oz cake crumbs
6 tbsp icing sugar
2 tbsp cocoa powder

1 Break the chocolate into pieces and place in a bowl with the butter. Set the bowl over a pan of gently simmering water. Stir until melted and combined.

2 Remove from the heat and beat in the rum. Stir in the desiccated coconut, cake crumbs and two-thirds of the icing sugar. Beat until combined. Add a little extra rum if the mixture is stiff.

3 Roll the mixture into small balls and place them on a sheet of baking paper. Leave to chill until firm.

4 Sift the remaining icing sugar on to a large plate. Sift the cocoa powder on to another plate. Roll half of the truffles in the icing sugar until coated and roll the remaining truffles in the cocoa powder.

5 Place the truffles in paper sweet cases and chill until required.

⭐⭐ easy

🕐 45 mins

🕐 5 mins

🎩 COOK'S TIP

Make the truffles with white chocolate instead of dark and replace the rum with coconut liqueur or milk, if you prefer. Roll them in cocoa powder or dip in melted milk chocolate.

Marzipan, honey and dark and milk chocolate are combined into little morsels of sheer delight.

Double Chocolate Truffles

1 Line 2 baking trays with baking paper. Beat together the butter and grated marzipan until thoroughly combined and fluffy. Stir in the honey, a little at a time, then stir in the vanilla essence.

2 Place the dark chocolate and 200 g/7 oz of the milk chocolate in the top of a double boiler or in a heatproof bowl set over a pan of barely simmering water. Stir over a low heat until melted and smooth. Remove from the heat and let it cool slightly.

3 Stir the melted chocolate into the marzipan mixture, then spoon the chocolate/marzipan mixture into a piping bag fitted with a large, round nozzle and pipe small balls on to the prepared baking trays. Leave to cool and set.

4 Put the remaining milk chocolate in the top of a double boiler or in a heatproof bowl set over a pan of barely simmering water. Stir over a low heat until melted, then remove from the heat. Dip the truffles, 1 at a time, in the melted chocolate to coat them, then texture some of them by gently tapping them with a fork. Place on the baking trays and leave to cool and set.

MAKES **60**

175 g/6 oz unsalted butter
100 g/3½ oz marzipan, grated
4 tbsp clear honey
½ tsp vanilla essence
200 g/7 oz dark chocolate, broken into pieces
350 g/12 oz milk chocolate, broken into pieces

✪✪✪✪ challenging
🕑 1 hr 25 mins
🕑 10 mins

The perfect pick-me-up on a cold winter's night, this delicious drink will get the tastebuds tingling.

Chocolate Eggnog

SERVES 4

8 egg yolks
200 g/7 oz sugar
1 litre/1¾ pints milk
225 g/8 oz dark chocolate, grated
150 ml/5 fl oz dark rum

1 Whisk the egg yolks with the sugar until pale and thickened.

2 Pour the milk into a large pan, add the grated chocolate and bring to the boil. Remove from the heat and gradually beat in the egg yolk mixture. Stir in the rum and pour into 4 heatproof glasses.

⭐ very easy

🕐 10 mins

🕐 5 mins

🍳 COOK'S TIP

Eggnog can also be made using brandy or whisky.

Brandy and chocolate have a natural affinity, as this richly flavoured drink amply demonstrates.

Hot Brandy Chocolate

1 Pour the milk into a pan and bring to the boil, then remove from the heat. Place the chocolate in a small pan and add 2 tablespoons of the hot milk. Stir over a low heat until the chocolate has melted. Stir the chocolate mixture back into the hot milk and add the sugar.

2 Stir in the brandy and pour into 4 heatproof glasses. Top each with a swirl of whipped cream and sprinkle with a little cocoa.

SERVES 4

1 litre/1¾ pints milk
115 g/4 oz dark chocolate, broken into pieces
2 tbsp sugar
5 tbsp brandy

to decorate
6 tbsp whipped cream
4 tsp cocoa powder, sifted

🍽 **COOK'S TIP**

You can vary this recipe by using rum, whisky or your favourite liqueur.

⭐ very easy
🕐 10 mins
🕐 7–10 mins

CHOCOLATE

Rich and soothing, a hot chocolate drink in the evening can be just what you need to help ease away the stresses of the day.

Hot Chocolate Drinks

EACH SERVES 2

spicy hot chocolate
600 ml/1 pint milk
1 tsp ground mixed spice
100 g/3½ oz dark chocolate
4 cinnamon sticks
100 ml/3½ fl oz double cream, whipped lightly

chocolate & orange toddy
75 g/2¾ oz orange-flavoured dark chocolate
600 ml/1 pint milk
3 tbsp rum
2 tbsp double cream
grated nutmeg

★ very easy
🕐 5 mins each
🕐 5 mins each

1 To make Spicy Hot Chocolate, pour the milk into a small pan. Sprinkle in the mixed spice.

2 Break the dark chocolate into squares and add to the milk. Heat the mixture over a low heat until the milk is just boiling, stirring constantly to prevent the milk from burning on the bottom of the pan.

3 Place 2 cinnamon sticks in each of 2 cups and pour in the spicy hot chocolate. Top with the whipped double cream and serve.

4 To make Chocolate & Orange Toddy, break the orange-flavoured dark chocolate into squares and place in a small saucepan with the milk. Heat the mixture over a low heat until just boiling, stirring constantly.

5 Remove the pan from the heat and stir in the rum. Pour into 2 cups.

6 Pour the cream over the back of a spoon or swirl on to the top so that it sits on top of the hot chocolate. Sprinkle with grated nutmeg and serve at once.

🍳 **COOK'S TIP**

Using a cinnamon stick as a stirrer will give any hot chocolate drink a sweet, delicate flavour of cinnamon without overpowering the flavour of the chocolate.

These delicious chocolate summer drinks are perfect for making a chocoholic's summer day!

Cold Chocolate Drinks

1 To make the Chocolate Milk Shake, pour about half of the ice-cold milk into a blender.

2 Add the drinking chocolate powder to the blender with 1 scoop of the chocolate ice cream. Blend until the mixture is frothy and well mixed. Stir in the remaining milk.

3 Place the remaining 2 scoops of chocolate ice cream in 2 serving glasses and carefully pour the chocolate milk over the ice cream.

4 Sprinkle a little cocoa powder (if using) over the top of each drink and serve at once.

5 To make the Chocolate Ice Cream Soda, divide the Glossy Chocolate Sauce equally between 2 glasses.

6 Add a little soda water to each glass and stir to combine the sauce and soda water. Place a scoop of ice cream in each glass and then top up with more soda water.

7 Place a dollop of whipped double cream on the top, if liked, and sprinkle with a little grated dark or milk chocolate.

🟤 **COOK'S TIP**

Served in a tall glass, a milk shake or an ice cream soda makes a scrumptious snack in a drink. Serve with straws, if wished.

EACH SERVES 2

chocolate milk shake
450 ml/16 fl oz ice cold milk
3 tbsp drinking chocolate powder
3 scoops chocolate ice cream
cocoa powder, to dust (optional)

chocolate ice cream soda
5 tbsp Glossy Chocolate Sauce (see page 75)
soda water
2 scoops chocolate ice cream
double cream, whipped (optional)
dark or milk chocolate, grated

⭐⭐ easy

🕐 5 mins each

🕐 15 mins each

Savouries

Chocolate may seem an unusual ingredient to use in savoury dishes, but Mexican cooks have long known about its wonderful affinity with chillies and red peppers. It can be used to add a fabulous new flavour to dishes that you may have normally cooked in a more traditional way. Chillies, red peppers and chocolate feature in two of the recipes in this section, Mole Poblano and Mexican Beef Stew. For a lighter dish that is also suitable for vegetarians, try the Nut and Chocolate Pasta. Finally, the Veal in Chocolate Sauce is perfect for a dinner party, where the chocolate will add an interesting flavour to this meat stew to surprise and satisfy you and your guests.

This great Mexican celebration dish, ladled out at fiestas, baptisms and weddings, is known for its combination of hot chillies and chocolate.

Mole Poblano

SERVES 4

3 mulato chillies
3 mild ancho chillies
5–6 New Mexico or California chillies
1 onion, chopped
5 garlic cloves, chopped
450 g/1 lb ripe tomatoes
2 tortillas, preferably stale, cut into
    small pieces
pinch of ground cloves
pinch of fennel seeds
pinch each of ground cinnamon, coriander
    and cumin
3 tbsp lightly toasted sesame seeds or tahini
3 tbsp flaked or coarsely ground
    blanched almonds
2 tbsp raisins
1 tbsp peanut butter (optional)
475 ml/16 fl oz chicken stock
3–4 tbsp grated dark chocolate, plus extra
    for garnishing
2 tbsp mild chilli powder
3 tbsp vegetable oil
salt and pepper
about 1 tbsp lime juice

✪✪✪   moderate
    1 hr 20 mins
    15 mins

1 Using metal tongs, toast each chilli over an open flame for a few seconds until the colour darkens. Alternatively, roast in an ungreased frying pan over a medium heat, turning constantly, for about 30 seconds.

2 Place the toasted chillies in a bowl or a pan and pour boiling water over to cover. Cover with a lid and leave to soften for at least 1 hour or overnight. Once or twice lift the lid and rearrange the chillies so that they soak evenly.

3 Remove the softened chillies with a slotted spoon. Discard the stems and seeds and cut the flesh into pieces. Place in a blender.

4 Add the onion, garlic, tomatoes, tortillas, cloves, fennel seeds, cinnamon, coriander, cumin, sesame seeds or tahini, almonds, raisins and peanut butter if using, then process to combine. With the motor running, add enough stock through the feeder tube to make a smooth paste. Stir in the remaining stock, chocolate and chilli powder.

5 Heat the oil in a heavy-based pan until it is smoking, then pour in the mole mixture. It will splatter and pop as it hits the hot oil. Cook for 10 minutes, stirring occasionally to prevent it from burning.

6 Season with salt, pepper and lime juice, garnish with grated chocolate and serve.

Colourful and richly flavoured, this stew is somewhat time-consuming, but well worth the effort.

Mexican Beef Stew

1 Arrange the red peppers on a baking tray and cook in a preheated oven, 240°C/475°F/Gas Mark 9, for about 20 minutes, until the skins have blackened and are beginning to blister. Using tongs, transfer them to a plastic bag. Tie the top and set aside.

2 Meanwhile, cut a cross in the skin on the base of the tomato. Put it in a bowl, cover with boiling water and let it stand for 1 minute. Remove the tomato from the water, then peel and seed it. Dice the tomato flesh, and put it into a food processor. When the peppers are cool enough to handle, peel and seed them, then chop the flesh. Add the peppers to the food processor, together with the onion, chocolate, garlic and vinegar. Process the ingredients to a purée.

3 Heat the oil in a flameproof casserole or large pan. Add the steak, in batches if necessary, and fry over a medium heat, stirring frequently, until browned all over. Season to taste with salt and pepper. Add the chocolate purée and beef stock. Tie the cloves and cinnamon in a small piece of muslin and add to the pan. Bring to the boil, then lower the heat, cover and simmer for 1–1¼ hours.

4 Add the carrots and potato to the pan, stir well and simmer for a further 30 minutes. Remove and discard the muslin bag. Taste the stew and adjust the seasoning if necessary. Garnish with the fresh coriander and serve immediately with cooked green vegetables, such as green beans.

SERVES 4

2 red peppers
1 beef tomato
1 onion, cut into quarters
55 g/2 oz dark chocolate, broken into pieces
2 garlic cloves, chopped roughly
3 tbsp red wine vinegar
3 tbsp vegetable oil
800 g/1 lb 12 oz lean braising steak, diced
salt and pepper
375 ml/13 fl oz beef stock
2 cloves
2.5-cm/1-inch piece of cinnamon stick
2 large carrots, finely chopped
1 large potato, diced
1 tbsp chopped fresh coriander, to garnish

★★★ moderate
🕐 15 mins
🕐 2 hrs 15 mins

This main course dish is popular in northern Europe, and makes an unusual and satisfying vegetarian supper.

Nut *and* Chocolate Pasta

SERVES 4

salt
350 g/12 oz dried ribbon pasta, such as
    tagliatelle or fettuccine
1 tsp butter, for greasing
2–3 tbsp fresh white breadcrumbs

sauce
6 tbsp butter
85 g/3 oz icing sugar
4 eggs, separated
85 g/3 oz ground roasted hazelnuts
85 g/3 oz dark chocolate, grated
4 tbsp fresh white breadcrumbs
½ tsp ground cinnamon
finely grated rind of ½ lemon

1 Bring a large pan of lightly salted water to the boil. Add the pasta and cook for 8–10 minutes or according to the instructions on the packet, until tender, but still firm to the bite. Drain, rinse under cold running water and set aside.

2 To make the sauce, beat together the butter, half the sugar and the egg yolks until frothy.

3 In a separate bowl, whisk the egg whites with the remaining sugar until stiff, then fold them into the butter mixture.

4 In another bowl, mix the hazelnuts, grated chocolate, breadcrumbs, cinnamon and lemon rind, then stir into the egg mixture. Add the pasta and stir gently to mix.

5 Grease an ovenproof dish with butter. Sprinkle with breadcrumbs, tapping lightly to coat the base and sides, then tip out any excess. Spoon the pasta mixture into the dish and bake in a preheated oven, 200°C/400°F/Gas Mark 6, for 25–30 minutes. Serve immediately, with roasted vine tomatoes (see Cook's Tip), if desired.

 COOK'S TIP

To roast vine tomatoes, put 12 small tomatoes in an ovenproof dish, sprinkle with 2 tablespoon olive oil, and season with salt and pepper to taste. Roast in a preheated oven, 200°C/400°F/Gas Mark 6, for 15–20 minutes.

✪✪✪   moderate

🕐   20 mins

🕐   35–40 mins

Chocolate can enrich stews based on a broad range of meats, including game, but it is important to be light-handed or it can become thick and cloying.

Veal *in* Chocolate Sauce

1 Heat 3 tablespoons of the oil in a large, flameproof casserole. Add the veal and cook over a medium heat, stirring, until lightly browned. Remove from the casserole and set aside. Add the onion, garlic, carrots, celery and chillies to the casserole and fry, stirring, for 5 minutes, until the onion is softened.

2 Stir in 300 ml/10 fl oz of the wine and all of the stock, and return the meat to the casserole. Add the thyme, bay leaf, juniper berries, cloves and cinnamon, and season with salt and pepper. Bring to the boil, stirring, then cook in a preheated oven, 200°C/400°F/Gas Mark 6, for 1 hour. Top up the casserole with more wine from time to time, if necessary.

3 Meanwhile, make a cross in the base of the chestnuts, put them on a baking tray, bake in the oven for 20 minutes, then shell them.

4 While the chestnuts are cooking, place the shallots in a small roasting tin and coat them with the remaining oil. Roast in the oven for 15–20 minutes, until golden and tender.

5 Remove the casserole from the oven and lift out the meat with a slotted spoon. Place it in a serving dish, add the chestnuts and shallots and keep warm. Strain the cooking juices into a clean pan. Discard the contents of the strainer. Set the pan over a medium heat, bring to the boil and cook until slightly reduced. Stir in the chocolate until melted and adjust the seasoning, if necessary. Pour the sauce over the meat, garnish with the parsley, and bay leaves if using, and serve.

SERVES 8

5 tbsp vegetable oil
675 g/1½ lb boneless veal (or pork), cut into 2.5-cm/1-inch cubes
1 onion, chopped
2 garlic cloves, chopped
2 carrots, chopped
2 celery sticks, chopped
2 fresh red chillies, deseeded and chopped
300–425 ml/10–15 fl oz red wine
125 ml/4 fl oz beef stock
2 tsp chopped fresh thyme
1 bay leaf
4 juniper berries, crushed lightly
2 cloves
2.5-cm/1-inch piece of cinnamon stick
salt and pepper
225 g/8 oz chestnuts
8 shallots, quartered
55 g/2 oz dark chocolate, grated

garnish
2 tbsp chopped fresh parsley
2 fresh bay leaves, optional

✪✪✪ moderate
🕐 20 mins
🕐 1 hr 45 mins

Index